NEVERLAND

Also by Vanessa Kisuule

Poetry

Joyriding the Storm
A Recipe for Sorcery

NEVERLAND

The Pleasures and Perils of Fandom

Vanessa Kisuule

CANONGATE

First published in Great Britain, the USA and Canada in 2024
by Canongate Books Ltd, 14 High Street, Edinburgh EH1 1TE

Distributed in the USA by Publishers Group West
and in Canada by Publishers Group Canada

canongate.co.uk

1

British Library Cataloguing-in-Publication Data
A catalogue record for this book is available on
request from the British Library

ISBN 978 1 83885 707 3

Typeset in Bembo Std by Palimpsest Book Production Ltd,
Falkirk, Stirlingshire

Printed and bound by CPI Group (UK) Ltd, Croydon CR0 4YY

CONTENTS

AUTHOR'S NOTE

Some of the events described in this book didn't happen. There are a few reasons why I chose to fictionalise these parts. Some experiences I wanted to explore involved loved ones who did not consent to having their darkest moments detailed in a book. This ethical choice then grew into something else, a creative wrestle with form that mirrored the challenges of the difficult themes. Frankly, it's fun to make things up. I didn't want to be constrained to the limits of direct experience, the tyranny of what poet Jack Underwood describes as 'realist anecdotalism'. While my memories inform much of the work, flights of fancy have stretched this book's capacity to places it couldn't have traversed otherwise.

I like to assume that most readers approach a book with the generosity it deserves. However, being born into my particular yet arbitrary skin suit: young(ish), black, female, blah, blah, blah, I am doomed to be read by some with intolerable earnestness. The media clamours for our testimony yet seems impervious to our intellectual choices. There is fun in the mischief to be had when the obligation to be instructive, literal or (god forbid) palliative is abandoned. My interest lies with the truth(s) in transgression, the 'why' over the 'what'.

I am not an authoritative voice. I am unreliable and chronically tangential. I am, alas, HOORAY, a hack. Lying can be its own form of violence, an abuse of implicit trust. So I have vowed to be honest about my own lies here and explain at least part of their function. The rest, of course, is yours to ponder on.

INTRODUCTION

I will never love
Anyone the way I love
My memories and their cliffs.
—Victoria Chang

For the latter end of my childhood and the initial bloom of adolescence, I was in a one-sided but deeply passionate relationship with Michael Jackson. If you feel creeped out by reading that sentence, then spare a thought for me, a grown woman, typing it. I'm writing this in the cooling magma of that obsession, one I happen to share with millions of others. I don't pretend to be an objective observer, some clear-eyed critic of celebrity worship and the psychic rot it signals. Please know I am deeply implicated. I was and am maddened by Michael. That madness fed me, made the outlines of my life sharper, its colours and sounds vivid as Eden. But I'm pretty sure that same madness cost me my conscience. This book is my attempt to understand why.

Expressing my love for Michael comes with its own choreography, a scatter of tics. *I was kind of obsessed*, I mutter, *still sort of am*, followed by a self-conscious smirk or shake of the head.

I use variations on this sentence every time. 'Kind of', 'sort of': qualifiers as desperate apologies. Even when given permission to speak honestly, I can never fully express the extent of my fixation, the gasping totality of it. It stoppers my throat and slows my tongue. People nod in response, offer their slightly bemused smiles. If they're kind, they'll share an anecdote on which Michael's shadow loosely hangs: watching 'Thriller' with their family on the TV, drunkenly dancing to 'Billie Jean' at weddings, scuffing their dress shoes as they squeak backwards across the floor.

By this, they mean: yes, he is there in my story, too. You are not alone. It's been said many times by many people, but I feel compelled to repeat it: no other musical artist, before or since, has made such an indelible mark on popular culture. You could walk the entire surface of the earth and fail to find a person who did not know his name and his music. For some, Michael is no more than a faint asterisk. For me, he was the nucleus. All things were informed and enriched by his existence. If I can feel deeply now, it's because I learnt how to truly commit, to marvel, to focus and worship, for him.

I was instructed by my religious family and Catholic schooling to worship Jesus, but it was Michael's shining form I followed. Church was one of a long list of obligations, sitting beside maths homework and the purgatory of house chores. I dreaded that heavy, humourless place, which seemed to be the very site of punishment it promised to save me from. Sure, the statues of Jesus in our school chapel did have their flashes of gold. When the light hit them just so, they had a promising glow. Sometimes, a more rousing hymn sent a muted thrill through my body. But Michael? Loving him felt instinctual and compelling, the rewards immediate and infinite. Being his fan felt like practice for some larger, undefined purpose, some ecstatic apex I assumed life would reach.

But as the impact of his music fades from the foreground and the delayed conversation about his alleged abuse of children grows in pitch, my fandom dries up at its corners. It is the pain of any once-devout worshipper who looks up at the sky to see the floor of heaven replaced by clouds. My hero betrayed me, and I don't know what to do. I have large, structural questions about hero worship and how it connects to violence, but underneath those is a small, restless child, reeling. Why does Michael still have this grip on her, on me?

Any attempts to remove Michael's music from our cultural lexicon haven't caught much traction. The haggard fossil of Michael's legacy remains, despite it all. It would seem that the music, the dancing and the memories are just too precious. But any joy we get from his music now is forever complicated. Speculative questions hover, sour the once-pleasing nostalgia his songs used to spark. Some may choose to tune these questions out, but now, more than ever, our cultural moment is seriously reckoning with what it means to separate the art from the artist. After years of campaigning from a few relentless individuals, R. Kelly was removed from all Spotify playlists, then finally charged and sent to jail for his systematic abuse of women and girls. In 2009, Chris Brown split open his girlfriend Rihanna's face after an awards show. When the news broke, the attack sent shockwaves through the media. It was unclear if Chris Brown's public reputation could weather the scandal. At the time of writing, Brown still tops the charts and sells out shows. Any smugness I feel at my capacity to 'boycott' Chris Brown's music is tempered. I love 'Forever' as much as any nostalgic millennial, but forgoing his music is no great sacrifice on my part. Unlike Michael, he is not integral to the landscape of my life. The stakes were low, the personal loss minimal. I think this lies at the heart of much of our moral decisions. We weigh up not just what we believe, but how much of our selfhood we would have to renegotiate. The bigger the shift, the stronger the reluctance to let go. Fearful of pulling a string that would unravel a whole structure, many of us avoid this work in favour of wilful, if not blissful, ignorance. Our condemnation is arbitrary and uneven, justice less of a scale and more a whimsical dance. But gone are the days where the abusive acts of famous stars were seen as a mere distraction from their genius.

We live in the age of the internet and its many boons and burdens. Yes, there is a ubiquitous misuse of therapy speak, broad strokes made on painfully complex topics. But there is also a greater inclination to believe people when they say the worst a human can do to them was done. I am glad to live in that world. It is safer for me, for all of us, if only in part. But this has come at a price. My ability to enjoy the work of certain artists will never again be frictionless. I no longer take for granted that people I love and who love me are inherently good or incapable of abhorrent acts. It's a price I've paid reluctantly, with no small amount of resistance and occasional fury.

At first, I thought this was a book that hinged on an 'if': whether the allegations were indisputably true. Somewhere, surely, lay the undeniable answer of 'what happened'. From there, I could plant both feet down on one side. I believed, naively, that this was about cold, hard facts. 'If only I could be sure, I would reason. If I just bent the spools of information at my disposal just so, I would know what to think, what to feel and then what to *do*. What worries me to the marrow is the matter of the Michaels we all live with and look up to, how willing we are to sacrifice our morals in service to their glittering image. There is a concrete reason I write this, rather than slipping all these thoughts into a locked drawer. The beginning point is me and Michael and the many people who have also found themselves obsessed to the point of unreason.

We coo and shudder at the public spectacle of scandal, watching the fallout from celebrity abuse cases as if they were thrilling TV dramas. We don't seem so interested in examining our own passivity, the parallels between these high-profile stories and the relational ruptures in our own lives. Celebrities are palpably separate from us, seeming to live on some alternative plane above the rest of us normals. They are more visible and more wealthy, symbols first and people second. But though we deify them, they are just like us in their foibles and failures. The only difference might be how their wealth and fame either insulates them from scrutiny or exacerbates its glare. This aside, the misbehaviour of a beloved celebrity often serves as an allegory for all of our shadowy social ills, and how we fail to look at them.

So this is also a book about our personal relationships and the private acts of interpersonal worship that can facilitate harm. What I wonder is not if we are this way, but why and how much. I want to know if there is anything better we can do than just ignore abuse or deduce that all its perpetrators are evil. The fact is there is no evil gene, no scientific evidence that unequivocally proves that some people are just born cruel. Evil is a story we created to appease ourselves of difficult, relational work. Contrary to popular opinion, I don't see humanising perpetrators as siding with them or excusing their behaviour. If we dismiss these people as 'evil', we are resigned to a cycle of widespread abuse that can only ever be punished once lives have already been ruined. I write all of this with the primary desire for less people to build lives in the long shadow of formative abuse.

When it came to it, I wanted my love for Michael to remain untarnished. For this, I muffled my disquiet. Michael was different to the others, I'd argue. Why? The reasons changed like weather. He was troubled, childlike, ambushed. Confused? Yes, he was confused. He was inappropriate with those kids, perhaps, but not sexual. I scripted versions of events that stopped just short of blatant horror. The harder I held onto him as the exception, the more untenable the farce became. What were my morals worth if I was so willing to bend them for the privilege of denial?

I can't do that any more.

My shame is a small fissure sitting to the left of my chest, and when I think of Michael it rattles. The shame is directly proportional to how deeply and sincerely I loved him. Look – I have trouble owning my tenses. I love him.

And by love, I mean own. I own him. And by him, I mean a specific, limited edition version of Michael Jackson™. The Michael that sat loyal and glowing in the passenger seat of my childhood. My companion and diligent babysitter, my mentor, my yardstick, my salve from boredom and loneliness. He was the world, which seemed bigger simply because he occupied it at the same time as me. He was the moon, an orbit, a gravitational contract.

But I didn't stay obsessed forever. Like most people as they get older, I developed other interests and allegiances. Being Michael's disciple was at odds with the person I was becoming, a person who wanted to make their own artistic mark, to hopefully fall in love with other artists and places and ways of being. There was no dramatic renouncing. It simply left me in layers, day by day, the ardour shrinking to a faded fondness. Sometimes, I mourn it. Where did it all go? The time consumed, the faith nurtured, the dance moves mimicked to slick perfection?

Now, I question and critique everything I ever assumed of Michael, my head busy with the real and assumed opinions of others. A free and foolish heart can't survive the questions I now live with. Sometimes I fumble through the dark of the past, hungry for that undiluted feeling. I want the weight and width of it back, all of its beauty and burden. I am jealous of my former self, her capacity for complete devotion and absorption. Naive and misguided as I was, I felt full, my heart's desire clear. I was alive.

As children, we learn about the neat splitting of the world. There are Good People and Bad People, the latter in the shadows and the former bathed in light. In fairy tales, each wears their designation in their physical form. Good People are not only beautiful but fluent in movement and speech. They are talented, artistic, move with the ease of winged creatures. Bad People are ugly, lonely and irredeemable, blighted by some unexplained absence of compassion. These positions are innate and immovable, not a matter of what they choose but what they are.

Ideally, as adults, we come to understand that anyone, including the people we love and revere, are capable of violating the human contract. The problem is many of us cannot accept this.

They said Michael, my Michael, touched little boys. I heard it many times. They wouldn't shut up about it, the papers and newscasters and the kids at school to boot. My brain didn't compute what it could not bear to carry. And now? Now I can just about state it without a quiver in my voice, without cushioning it with caveats or rebuttals. But it's still hard to claim the thought as my own. In defiance of received wisdom, time did not make this any easier. It only seemed to get heavier. How could I claim to have any integrity when I kept succumbing to this hurdle? And so Michael became the morality tale that would test my mettle. If my ethics are anything more than ornamental, this is where I prove it.

We are allowed to be disgusted at violent perpetrators. We are justified in our rage and paranoia, our fear and vengefulness. Until recently, I believed the solution to sexual violence was clear: rounding up all the rapists, locking them up and hurling the key into the ocean. If other inmates saw fit to beat them to a pulp, I felt no sorrow or pity at their fate. It was, I felt, a brute but necessary justice.

But this addresses the aftermath of abuse, not its root. At the end of our tears and balled fists, our appeals to courts and prisons and YouTube conspiracy theorists, what is left? I have reached an impatience with this blunt thinking, how incurious we are about the mindset of an abuser. This is not just out of morbid curiosity, but so we might be less seduced by the self-serving lies we tell ourselves. All of us, at some point, have justified some hurt we have caused or ignored. It's important to discuss these topics not from some rhetorical wonderland where people behave in the clear, prescriptive ways we wish them to. I've endeavoured to discuss people as I believe they are: inescapably flawed and contradictory yet always capable of making better choices.

I am working with the base assumption that it's hard and constant work to be a good person. It is not an innate disposition but a series of decisions that aren't always easy or gratifying. I don't believe in a utopia where any of us can ensure we would never commit a heinous act against another person. This book is intended as the literary equivalent of a squirm. I'm not interested in placating anybody, least of all myself. It's only fair that I put myself through the rigorous critique I ask of others, no matter how uncomfortable. I want to know how I, you, we, are complicit in the cycle, especially when the perpetrator is someone we collectively revere. If it isn't Michael, it might be Morrissey or Marilyn Manson. It's our friends and parents, our teachers and beloved partners. It might even be you, wilfully oblivious reader, assuring yourself this is a book concerning the troubling behaviour of others, when perhaps a long, hard look at your own conduct is due.

The private decision of whether to separate the art from the artist is only part of the equation. Beyond this personal quandary is a wider, more pressing one. When news hits that a celebrity has been found to be abusive, we need to be better at seeing them as symptoms of a wider pestilence of violence to which we all contribute. More often than not, abuse proliferates unchecked because we are stuck in our own disbelief, our desperate need to keep our regard for our favourite stars intact.

This book starts with Michael, then veers into other pop-star fixations I've had over the years. So many of them! They stack themselves like dominoes, cascading into each other. Each brief dalliance, in its way, stems from the original, presses the same pleasure points. All roads in my mind seem to stem from Michael and lead back to him, too. It's dazzling, the gamut he covers, how he's burrowed his way into every aspect of my life. There he is, in foundational family anecdotes and feverish diary entries. I have stalked him across every dance floor I've hit, every mouth I've kissed. I have invented fictional people and alternative universes to see if the answer to my questions is hiding beneath some rip in the space–time continuum.

Coming to terms with obsession and looking it in the eye is the first port of call, looking coolly at its irrational heat and bluster. We fixate on someone not because we are weak, but because we long to surrender to something bigger than ourselves. It's tempting to empty the grab bag of blame and roll out some easy scapegoats: the nihilistic haze of secular living, capitalism and its anti-human imperatives, our material conditions exponentially improving while our 'why' remains elusive. And still, having lived amongst each other for millennia, we are largely stumped on what love might look like as a social practice. We are addicted to the sensation but don't think seriously about its mechanics. Love has become a catch-all term for warm, fuzzy feelings, rather than a code of conduct. Yet the language of hate and violence is well-developed, spoken and understood by all of us. If only we could chalk this up to malice. It is infinitely more interesting, and devastating, that many people believe their violence *is* an act of love. This is human nature and we will never be free of it entirely. But it could be better, I think. It's important to believe it could be better. What other choice do we have?

Monsters Under the Bed

Some nights, I'm beset with fears I cannot shake. They are not the legitimate fears of a young woman living alone in the city. I don't worry about serial killers climbing through my window or being burgled at gunpoint. Instead, I'm beset with visions of gremlins and killer clowns, the antagonists from stories told by tired parents to antsy children.

I do what I'd make my Uncle do for me as a kid when I couldn't sleep: tuck myself into the duvet so no part is exposed to the air. With my body tight against the sheets, I am snug as sausage meat swaddled in pastry. The edges of my panic soften a little. I lie still, scared of breaking the cocoon.

The monster under my bed shapeshifts, taking on many faces and voices. I fear if I relax too much as I fall asleep, a foot might loll out beside the mattress. The monster will take me by the ankle, drag my body down to its hungry underworld. It is patient, but I am vigilant. I remain half awake, fitful and alert.

I've been taught to fear the thugs and murderers and rapists, bloodthirsty people who subsist on people like me, the neutral and innocent. But these days I am visited by thoughts of myself under the bed. What if I were the monster? The thought is distressing at first, then oddly invigorating. My fear is usurped by a morbid curiosity, something like peeling back the plaster on an unhealed cut. It strikes me that it is no life, to be mummified by fear. Better to throw the covers from my sweating body and look under the bed, meet the monster not with threats, but questions.

An Evolving Definition of Obsession

Obsession was once a considered pursuit. You had to work for every morsel of information. Total and ever-growing knowledge of your idol was the prize; time, money and cunning were the tools. When I was young, that meant constant trips to the library, an occasional book begged for as a present, bought with pocket money, or, as a last measure, stashed under the arm at the local Waterstones praying not to set off the door alarms. I'd spend my precious, allocated hour on the massive library computers watching videos, printing lists of trivia at 10p a page. These days you need only type in a name to a search bar and there it all is: reams of seamless, unearned information sorted by date, relevance and niche interest. To join a fan club, you once had to handwrite a request, seal it in an envelope, lick a stamp and walk to your nearest post box to send it. If such a club didn't exist, it was your responsibility to start it. To be a fan was hard, earnest work! Not so much these days, or at least not in the same way.

I am the dullest kind of Luddite, I know. But I have to name this weary curmudgeon that lives between my ribs. She ashes her cigarette, heaves a sigh and shakes her wizened head. *Obsessives ain't what they used to be*, she drawls. She can't relate to this new crop of internet Stans. She resents and envies their camaraderie, the ease of access to their beloved stars. Everything I had of Michael I bought, begged or borrowed. There was always something furtive in my constant hunt for anything Michael related. The parts of him offered on the TV and radio were par for the course, nowhere near enough to quell my endless appetite. I read official and unofficial biographies, all crammed with variations on a life story I'd come to know as intimately as my own. Like the Hail Marys at church, I would repeat the litany of facts I'd learnt:

Date of birth: 29th August 1958

Place of birth: Gary, Indiana

Height: 5'9"

Records sold: 500 million and counting

What I hoped to do with this trivia is hard to qualify. Did I think he would show up at my house and quiz me, befriend me if I got a perfect score? It wasn't enough for the music to just wash over me, to sit, mouth agape, as he sang and danced behind a screen. Knowing these things about him gave me immense pride. Learning his life was the only way I knew to communicate my admiration, to make my love something active and muscular. There was, I assumed, some mystical tally in the sky keeping tabs on these rituals of mine. Surely, I was accumulating favour and good graces. Though I had many conversations with him in my head, I never wrote him any fan mail, unsure where I might send it or if it would reach him. He functioned like any imaginary friend might in the mind of a child. I just happened to share my friend with the rest of the world.

There were limits to how far I was willing to go. Some things I simply didn't have the resources or imagination for. I didn't, for example, camp outside hotels during any of his tours, or take a pilgrimage to the Neverland Ranch. There were fans who followed him around the world, spent every bit of money they had on gigs and merchandise. An Argentinian fan named Leo Blanco has spent over $44,000 dollars on cosmetic surgery to look like Michael. Unfortunate, then, that without heavy make-up he looks more like an underslept Joan Jett. It's easy for me to mock these fans, but I can see the slight deviations in my life story that might have made me a similar brand of uber-fan. My theory, for what it's worth, is that their level of fixation is a form of contagion. These are fans that seek each other out and egg each other on, making devotion into a shared hobby and competitive sport. I'm glad I didn't fall that deep or that far, but I think that was less a choice and more a circumstantial quirk.

In an online world where anything less than feverish ardour is met with crickets, everyone appears to be obsessed with everything at all times. Beauty editors write columns claiming to be 'obsessed' with this face cream or that mohair cardigan. Social media natives post clips from TV shows, songs and books and caption them 'LITERALLY OBSESSED'. For all this effusive froth, the overall effect is deadening. I don't think a lot of the people who use the word really mean it, which is not an offence in and of itself. But it does strike me as an insult to language and the full range of our emotions that we reach for the extreme even when our feelings are more layered or muted. This is the virulent, deadpan irony of the overstimulated and perpetually underwhelmed. What we consume in this landscape feels secondary to the demand to respond intensely to what we see, whether we feel strongly or not. But caps lock and superlatives cannot compensate for true intensity.

All of this online hyperbole feels like a wilful massaging of sentiment, the expression of feeling in its conspicuous absence. But this ritual is a thin mask for our restlessness. What does it mean to be obsessed when our attention is scissored to ribbons? We have more tools to aid and abet our private fixations than any other generation, yet there's less space to focus on or dedicate yourself to any one thing. That freakish focus still exists, but it has undoubtedly changed shape.

Obsession is hunger. Under it lies the faint yet constant threat of violence. Like addiction, it creates giddy feedback loops of euphoria and remorse. Obsession parts the fog of everyday life, offers a clear and fixed focus. But not all obsessions are created or treated equally. We reward certain cycles and sites of obsession over others: most potently, the mercenary fixations of hedge-fund managers and business tycoons, whose Machiavellian pursuit of money is accepted with equal awe and resignation. On the other side are those whose obsessions don't generate wealth or prestige. Indeed, their obsessions deplete their own resources, stealing their money, time and grip on reality. The single-minded mindset of the CEO is lionised, while the obsessive rituals of those we disdain – shrieking fan girls, especially – are deemed pathological and frivolous. In a neat and vicious cycle, it's the former category who build cultural empires funded by the latter.

Obsession is distinct from love in subtle but crucial ways. It constantly attempts to best itself, never satisfied with what it has. Now that the man himself cannot generate more music or intrigue, I am left with recycled interviews and songs, the compulsive resuscitation of a dying joy. Sometimes, it finds me again, unexpectedly. A song I haven't listened to in months returns, almost fresh; a syncopation or riff I hadn't noticed before works its charm. Then I am back again, justifying the sickness, conjuring more material to prove something I'm not sure I believe in any more. It's not him I am mourning. It's the lost belief, that smothering hush of firm faith. It's akin, I imagine, to the self-lacerating rituals after a break-up. Poring over old pictures and listening to playlists heavy with memories, sniffing a hoodie that holds some faint ghost of a once loved smell. This may seem a crass comparison, the latter being grief for an actual relationship and the former the shedding of a parasocial fantasy. But onto everyone we encounter, we project our hopes and neuroses. Much of our relationships, whether one-sided or mutual, occur inside the cinema of our minds, accessible to no one but ourselves.

When it came to accepting the idea that Michael, my Michael, had done the things they said on the news, I wish I could at least say the thought was pushed away with force. But there was nothing to digest or deny. The information simply boomeranged back to its source. It did not, would not, register. Because if Michael could do that, then what did that mean for . . .? And did that mean that . . .? How would I . . .? The thoughts couldn't bear their own conclusions, so I hid them somewhere dark and far away where I could not reach them.

No. It is worse than that. Forgive me, but I did not want to let go of my delusions. I did not even try.

CHILDHOOD

Track 1: Spit Shine The CD

My one-year-old godson, G, loves when his mother and I sing to him. Specifically, he loves when we sing classic garage hits. He is partial to 'Sweet Like Chocolate' and 'Flowers' and squeals with glee when I deliver my (flawless) rendition of Alesha Dixon's rap verse from Mis-Teeq's underrated single 'All I Want'.

One day we are listening to an eighties hits radio station and sing along to 'Billie Jean'. I snarl, grunt, grab my crotch, do a shaky spin on the crumb-strewn floor. He doesn't pick up these references, but not too many years from now he will.

He claps and gurgles, his doughy limbs all wriggle and rhythm. I think: *it begins*. Whether the song itself is pleasing him or he is just mirroring the excited gurn of my face, I don't know. But it's remarkable to be there for this, his first interaction with Michael. Everything is blissfully deferred. He knows nothing of him as image or symbol, hero or monster. His tongue can't even form the phonetics that shape his name: *my-call*. The moment, gone even as it happens, is kinetic fizz.

This is the most potent part of the Fantasy Parenting Montage, isn't it? I am drunk off my power, newly qualified to bestow the building blocks of taste on the porous youth! There are the tantrums and late nights and flung spoons of vegetable goo, but also this: handing down the music you love to a child you love, a relic of your psychic landscape that might take pride of place in theirs, too.

I'd like to feel it one more time, whatever my first listening experience was. The physical impact of music rearranging my body. It feels painfully distant now, a memory of a memory, an echo. I try to plug the gap with language, but the words scuttle around in their analytic dance, reaching prematurely for whys and hows. If I am to trace my first experiences of Michael, I want to go at it with my teeth. Sense first, thought second.

I reach twenty-two years back: to a summer holiday. Scratchy duffel bag in boot, carriageway grey as sky. Restless FM crackle. Au-to-glass-re-PAIR-au-to-glass-re-PLACE. Kent becomes London. Yellow foam blooms from cracks in car seats. Have you considered switching your car insurance? Head leant against glass. Hair grease smear makes watercolour of streets.

Rat-a-tat-tat, synthesiser drums. Volume dial turned until the car shakes. Mum's fingers tap steering wheel. *Saidyouwannabe-startinsumthin*. Chorus moreish as popcorn. The song fades and other things with it.

Slower now, down cul-de-sac. Cars slot neat along driveways. Wheels crunch against ground. A bungalow. Squat, like god's hand squashed it down. Pebbledash sandpapers palms. Charity shop smell in the hallway. Auntie answers the door in paisley headscarf, face peppered with moles. Uncle lifts his huge fist, signet ring winks. Waits for my knuckles to meet his. Familiar song calling from lounge. *Mama se mama sa ma ma coo sa*. Are you hungry? Auntie says. Always. Produce rustling gift of blue bag. Auntie's face splits open. A smile.

This is where I would stay for most of the long summer break as a kid. There wasn't much else to do but listen to music, so that's what we did. Auntie E's collection took up two sides of the lounge from floor to ceiling, with two whole CD racks and a smooth, conker-brown cabinet stuffed with records and cassettes. I liked the furred edges of the vinyl sleeves, how the cassettes spooled their ribbon guts if you pulled at them, though I knew there'd be consequences for doing so. It felt like she had a whole shop's worth of music in that room, a song for every waking hour with plenty more to spare. It all hinted at a large, sprawling world waiting for me, a mystic inheritance. I took for granted I would eventually hear it all, every single song in that bungalow and then the world. I would crack open the secret of every song's wisdom and stow it away for safekeeping.

Michael and I had no formal introduction. No one placed his CD in the player with ritualistic gravitas. No announcement, no slow-motion needle drop, no singular moment I can point to and say: that, reader, was the first time I heard him. Believe me, I am deeply unsatisfied by this narrative sagginess. That said, it's nothing a sprinkle of creative licence couldn't address for the purposes of this book. All of which is to say that Michael's influence, like many things that would come to be pivotal and devastating in my life, was not instantaneous. He moved like ink through water until, one day, I found that he had coloured everything. I struggle to recall a time before him, his music, his presence. Michael always was. Michael is.

My favourite album of his has changed countless times over the years. At the beginning, though, *Off The Wall* reigned supreme. It's a disco record, after all, and I liked anything that made my body shimmy and wiggle of its own accord. I played my aunt's copy so much that the opening track, 'Don't Stop 'Til You Get Enough', began to skip. Michael's opening roar got stuck in a looped stutter, the song's drop suspended just before the horns came in. Auntie, to her credit, didn't give me the bollocking I deserved for this. Instead, she showed me how to spit shine a CD. I enjoyed launching thick pellets of saliva onto the disc, smoothing its surface with the edge of my T-shirt. If I squinted, sometimes I could see the scratches, thin swipes that looked as though an angry cat had gone at it with its claws.

My silent, competitive pledge to myself was to one day have a CD collection vaster than Auntie's. I would start with every Michael album, of course, bought in reverential order: *Off The Wall*, *Thriller*, *Bad*, *Dangerous*, *HIStory* (even *Invincible*, why not). I would guard them from smears and scratches, keep the liner notes tucked sweetly in their sleeves. I took deep comfort in how CD cases stacked on top of each other, each case firm as vertebrae. Sometimes it felt like it was the CDs alone that held the room together. It amused me to think that, if they were removed, the whole bungalow would fall open like a flatpack box. To this day, I can't for the life of me remember what colour the walls were.

When I walked into HMV, I knew what I wanted. It was 1999, the threat and thrill of the Millennium Bug looming. But more importantly I was eight, which was basically ten, which was basically grown. Having got a copy of *Off The Wall* for Christmas, I was there for the next on my list: *Thriller*. I loved everything about the video: the reliable spike of fear as the camera panned to Michael's zombie face, the dance break in the middle, the black piping on the lapels of his red, red jacket. In my green velcro wallet were three crisp fivers. It usually contained shrapnel and sometimes, if I was lucky, the occasional two-pound coin. But never notes. That day, my pockets were padded and my mission clear.

But I didn't buy a copy of *Thriller*, at least not at this particular moment. Something else distracted me. A CD with a pale pink cover, a young girl on the front with her hands clasped in the shape of prayer: *...Baby One More Time* by Britney Spears. I could confidently replay every frame of the music video in my head: the impatient tapping of her fluffy pen on the school desk, the synchronised high kicks, the girl gang running down the corridor in their long socks and chunky leather shoes. I declined the cashier's offer of a bag and clasped the CD to my chest the whole bus ride home. I kept sneaking glances at it, to remind myself that it was real and it was mine.

Things I didn't know then: Britney was propaganda, the latent wet dream of modern America. White. Blonde. Southern. A disposition sweet enough to rot molars. She was sent to stoke embers of adoration and low-level failure in girls like me, and she succeeded. Physically and culturally, I could not relate to her in the slightest, living as she did across an ocean I couldn't name. She sang about a loneliness strong enough to kill, which sounded delicious and exhausting. But the lyrics were secondary to those melodies, so hummable and addictive. I knew nothing about love then, and I don't know much more now. As a child bereft of my own experiences, I took this testimony of love as painful waiting game and accepted it as prophecy. Maybe love was supposed to hurt, if it made music that good.

Buying her album was my first investment in music of the moment, a way to distinguish myself from the cultural hand-me-downs of my family. But somehow, my stern mother grew fond of '...Baby One More Time'. I'd hear her singing the chorus under her breath as she busied herself about the house, which pleased and annoyed me in equal measure. But she certainly didn't approve of Britney's provocative shimmies to the camera, or that tiny keyhole of flesh between her waistband and tied shirt. I paid particular attention to these moments that bewitched me and worried my mother. I began to thrill at the thought of doing the forbidden for its own sake, of using the blunt instrument of my body to shock. If Michael introduced me to magic, then Britney introduced me to danger. For all her ostensible sweetness and light, she had been sent to lead me astray.

When I closed my eyes and silently mimed along, I truly believed it: I *was* Britney. Her silky hair was tickling my shoulders; my arms, legs and feet were hers, my torso morphed from soft, brown and round to long, taut and tan. How I hated being pulled away from that private fantasy by my mother yelling at me to get ready for school or hoover the stairs. Behind my eyelids, I could see the crowds, their beaming faces and bright banners, the gleam of sweat on their foreheads. But I couldn't daydream myself out of my cheap market clothes, my rotund pre-teen body, my fractured, fatherless family. I was a child again, impotent, foolish, cursed to wear my school skirt at regulation length and my shirt sensibly tucked in.

This intense Britney phrase was retreading of familiar ground. In the early throes of my Michael fixation, I reached for the easiest forms of imitation I could find. In lieu of sounding or moving like him, an aim I continually reached for and missed, I dressed like him instead. I would leave the house with a woollen winter glove on one hand, lamenting its lack of sequins. In homage to the white tape Michael wrapped round his fingertips, I would wrap mine in beige coloured plasters stolen from the bathroom cabinet. On one slow evening when my mother was at work, I went over the plasters with a Tippex pen. For the rest of the week, it peeled off in tiny flecks that shed on the sofa and the carpet, left bits in my hair that looked like dandruff. Mum made me chase them with our cheap vacuum cleaner that wheezed and huffed but never picked much up.

I was a half-baked mimic, confined by whatever odds and ends I could repurpose in the house. But I loved the ritual, the pious feeling of kinship it gave me. It was a secret language Michael and I shared, a smoke signal I assumed he could pick up. Unlike with Britney, looking like him wasn't the aim. There was no appeal to the thought of inhabiting his pale, gangly body. It was his otherworldliness I wanted to borrow, the sameness of school and home I wished to escape. As far as I could tell, the adults around me were miserable, perpetually stressed and sullen. Only when music was playing did they seem to wake up from their stupor. They became themselves again when songs from their youth played loud and long into the night. Already, I was offended by my small little life and its earthly disappointments. I wanted out. I wanted more.

I would see this same hubris in the churn of naive hopefuls on *The X Factor* throughout the early noughties. God, I loved that stupid show! Every week, a hapless string of contestants delivered the same stock phrases to the camera. 'Since I was little, I've dreamed of being a star,' they all said. It was remarkable how little variation there was in their phrasing, the predictable beats of their life stories. The pantomime of pining unfolds like so:

Shot 1: [insert name] walks through the faded glory of their local pier with their hands in their pockets, stoic expression of war veteran.

Shot 2: [insert name] wanders through their rough council estate kicking at broken glass (which is a metaphor, by the way).

Shot 3: [insert name] sips at a pint, strolls up to karaoke machine, opens mouth.

A good singing voice was redemption. Redemption from poverty, boredom, ugliness, the nag of existential dread. Almost always, each contestant expressed bemusement at how, despite their talents, they were stuck working at a call centre or the bookies or the fish counter at Asda. This was not the dream promised by New Labour and *Smash Hits* magazine. On they came in their droves to collect the debt owed them. They all believed or hoped themselves special, yet the show chewed them all down into one pulsing blob of aimless want.

Despite the high chances of failure and public embarrassment, every year contestants willingly signed up for the circus. I believed in the show's transformative power, its seductive myths of social value and upward mobility. The message was clear: if your talent isn't co-signed by the masses, it has failed to serve its purpose. It may as well not exist. Living and working as most people do was a hideous fate to be avoided at all costs.

Like millions of British TV viewers, I compulsively watched

the cycle of brief fame and lingering irrelevance that awaited most of the contestants. It took me longer than it should have to see them as the cautionary tales they were. I felt confident that if I were on the show, I'd fare differently. I imagined what I would sing if I auditioned. My ideal outfit changed, but often I settled on a slinky halter top in a bright colour, embroidered jeans with heeled leather boots. Simon Cowell would call me 'world class'. I would be too rich and too important to hoover flecks of Tippex from the marble floor of the gorgeous mansion I lived in. Mum would have a matching one on the left-hand side, Uncle and Auntie E on the other.

It feels important to say that I was an only child until I was thirteen. It suited me fine, I think. Who's to say? I haven't lived the alternative version of my life where I wasn't, so it's impossible to compare. But with no siblings to play or squabble with and a single mother who had to work (and work and work), I learnt to fill entire days with elaborate worlds of my own making, worlds that were largely peopled by the famous figures I admired. Michael's was a world of colour and sparkle and camp, of choral swells that made the dullest moment into a movie. I replayed his songs and videos, panning for some new pleasure or surprise and always found something new.

Without him, I suspect the jaws of inertia would have closed around me. I think I'd have been very sad because there was a lot to be sad about. I see now that I was lonely, though not in some especially marked way. It seems to me that it's never a question of if we are lonely, but to what degree and what shape that loneliness takes. With Michael, I could build a full and busy world where difficult thoughts grew quiet.

First it was Michael, then Britney – a rotating cast of stars whose style I borrowed. There was my thankfully brief love affair with striped ties over vests, my homage to Avril Lavigne. When Janelle Monáe released 'Tightrope', I misspent many hours ironing my hair into a quiff so thin and gauzy the sun would pierce right through it. It's a calling card of youth, adopting the style of others in the hope we might stumble on some authentic notion of self along the way. The distinction between looking like and being like was lost on me. I spun through many cycles of brief joy that flattened into disaffection. Any effect won by imitation wore off too quickly. Always, I arrived back at the inescapable fact of myself.

Still, I hoped a time would come when this gap between the ideal and the reality would merge. One day, finally, there would be no unease, no nagging sense of unfulfilled destiny. Surely, that was what being grown up meant: the total absence of doubt. That I should have enjoyed this brief interim of trial and error, and the safety of doing so away from the gaze of a vicious public, is obvious in hindsight. But it's hard to ring-fence that time in our lives, for it to remain untouched by the rush to grow up and out and into the spotlight. This is why giving advice to the young is largely pointless. It is an act of self-soothing for the giver, who is really speaking to their former self in vain.

Interlude #1 – Sheila's Lament

Sliding your obligatory wince to the side, imagine an eighteen-year-old Britney Jean Spears stark naked except for a flesh-coloured G-string. You are not in trouble, nor are you conjuring anything you haven't been asked to before. Her pale skin is covered in a layer of talcum powder. The room is private, the only eyes privy to the scene are those of the scrupulous woman whose job is to handle costume, and you.

Britney's arms are folded across her chest. Whether this is down to the air con or a sudden surge of shyness, who knows or cares? The other woman in the room, let's call her Sheila, holds up a Britney-shaped garment, a gelatinous mould of cherry-red PVC. This piece of casing goes from neck to ankle. It will not wrinkle or slouch on any part of her body, the powder makes sure of that. It will also stop her from slow cooking under the lights and fire cannons dotted around the studio.

Sheila glances over Britney's frame. She is mildly concerned, but mostly envious. All that lovely, lithe body and not a clue what to do with it, she thinks.

The day she turned thirty-six, Sheila cut her hair short and dyed it a dark, decisive brown. It doesn't do to fight the inevitable. Oddly, her feet were the first to betray her. They spilled out, flat and wide like a platypus. She threw out all her summer sandals, recalling her mother's orthopaedic shoes, the slug-coloured soles that supported her aching arches. Footwear and contraceptive all in one. She'd felt a faint sorrow for her then, robbed of the option to wear pretty, impractical shoes that criss-cross over the skin like a corset. Not once did it occur to her that she was watching the future, her future, the place where all women end up eventually.

One foot then the other, Sheila says with a smile, prompting Britney to step into the costume. Her feet snake through the leg holes and peek back out. She wiggles her toes like a child does, for the sake of the sensation, a reminder of a dexterous body. Sheila feels like she is being mocked.

She misses being honked at in the street. The irritation she sometimes felt then seems silly now. Wasteful, even. She took for granted that her body would always be worthy of comment, wished she could mute the ones she liked and lean into those she did. Now she walks in silence knowing she won't be bothered and it bothers her. She still has her eyes, grey-green and fringed with long lashes, but eyes are not what make a man fling a marriage proposal from his window.

The zip's teeth nip at Britney's spine twice. She inhales sharply but otherwise doesn't protest. The catsuit is tight, squeaks in its crannies.

No way I'd let Jess out the house like that, Sheila's husband Jeff says. They are eating lamb chops for dinner, matching trays across their laps. Sheila's jaw works harder at the gristle in her mouth as Britney does a sultry grapevine across the screen. Jeff pretends to be disgruntled, but Sheila sees it, the shift in his posture, the glazed eyes of a man hypnotised.

But she isn't annoyed that her husband is ogling a girl young enough to be his daughter while pushing the dinner she cooked around his plate. It's his empty moralising that makes her face hot. Can't a young woman be allowed to enjoy her beauty while she has it? Must she be responsible for the wayward thoughts in any and every man's head? She changes the channel, remembering their first date together. When she got up to walk to the ladies' room, she did not look back once but she knew Jeff's eyes were on her. She'd never felt more powerful before or since.

I think of Sheila on set, dabbing on Britney's make-up and mopping her brow between takes, adjusting that red catsuit so it moulds perfectly to her body. I think of the issue of *Rolling Stone* that featured a seventeen-year-old Britney posing in a black bra top and polka dot underwear, a Teletubby soft toy tucked under her arm. 'Inside The Heart, Mind and Bedroom of a Teen Dream' the headline read. How many adults saw and signed off on this?

She looks over her shoulder at the photographer with that disturbingly knowing look that young girls learn reads as confidence. I taught myself from a young age, too, with my mother's wardrobe mirror as my accomplice. Britney would later defend her choice to pose this way, and it's unfair to rob Britney of her agency, partial and poisoned though it was. More importantly, I have yet to see an interview with the cameramen, the journalists at *Rolling Stone* or Sheila. Why are we not asking the adults to defend their choices?

★

Britney is a woman now. Her shadowed eyes betray the cost of fame, her fashion sense firmly trapped in the late nineties. Her stomach, still dutifully tanned and toned, is exposed above low-rise shorts. She swishes her bleached, beach-tousled hair. She dances for her millions of Instagram followers in her marble-floored living room. No one quite knows what to make of it. Her repetitive, eerily sexless moves inspire equal parts concern and disdain in the comments. I watch her, and admonish myself for watching her.

I recall a conversation with my friend Maya, who has a brand of swashbuckling ethics I both resent and envy. Vanessa, she declares, child stardom should be illegal. I am affronted, thinking of all we would lose to this: skinny little Stevie Wonder playing 'Fingertips' on his harmonica, the canonical early work of the Olsen twins, *Home Alone*, adorable, button-nosed Michael singing 'ABC' in a purple fedora.

There's one particular video I would hate to lose to this world free of child stars. It's an old clip of nine-year-old Britney singing a duet with Justin Timberlake on *The Mickey Mouse Club*. They both beam big smiles, shoulders manically bopping to a reggae-pop soundtrack. Justin's head looks tiny above his slouchy vest and baggy trousers. He fires off a terrible rap in something adjacent to patois. I should be irritated, but instead I find myself shipwrecked on an island of hopeless endearment. I ought to be sickened and disturbed at this, the tacit exploitation of children for profit. But they are so shiny, so brimful of promise. I suspect I have the spotlight fetish of a stage mum. Small mercy, then, that I've no children to impress this urge upon.

Britney's moves are the same as those she did in her heyday, the same my friends and I copied in the playground. Only now we have moved on, conceded to what women past a certain age are no longer meant to do. But now past forty, Britney still spins on the spot like a crazed dervish. Michael used to spin like that, too, until he became a blur of static. It's as if she hopes she can reset time if she just keeps spinning and spinning. She is stuck in a loop and so am I. I lie on the sofa watching her, the warm slab of my phone the only light left in the darkening room, my mind a long, narrow well of an echoing melody. I watch the clip one more time, one more time, one more—

Out of the well a man emerges, slick as if straight from a god's oesophagus. He is white. Average build, average height, hair a noncommittal mix of dirty blond and brown. His name is Max Martin, the hit-maker behind Britney's debut single '…Baby One More Time'. When he wrote it, he was twenty-seven years old. At the time of recording, Britney was sixteen. Of his uncanny skill for writing pop hits it was once said: 'In the last 20 years, no composer in the world has written melodies as sustainable or as widespread.' What does it mean for pop music to be sustainable? It must weather the elements of cultural and geographical difference, wielding a subtle campaign of dominance. The melodies must be self-sustaining and self-explanatory, as familiar the first time you hear them as the fiftieth.

Max Martin also wrote the song that soundtracked a swoon of house parties where girls mashed jaws with each other, newly aware of the currency of bi-curious cosplay. At parties, the surly bassline of 'I Kissed A Girl' would creep through the room as a few intrepid girls would pair up and make out. The year was 2008 and attitudes to queerness were at a strange impasse. A gestural tolerance had spread through mainstream culture by this point. Still, there were no openly gay kids at any of the four secondary schools I attended. When the girls started snogging to Katy Perry, the spectacle was met with knowing smirks and feral cheers. We'd point and gape like we were at the aquarium, the girls suddenly mystical as two-headed mermaids. They laughed into each other's mouths, fingers forking through tangled hair. Over their shoulders they caught our gaze and giggled, made sure we were watching.

I would be stood to the side, gripping an alcopop by the neck. The boys would jostle for view, smugly slap each other's backs as if they were somehow auteurs of the scene. The whole thing felt hollow, yet another bid for their skittish attention. Boys! Why did everything have to revolve around them? I was insanely jealous, of course. Not because I had any desire to kiss girls but because I wanted to do girlhood 'properly', partake in the rites of passage reserved for a beautiful, popular young woman in her prime.

Alternative forms for that song: a Trojan horse. A story within a story, one in which I don't feature. God knows desire is hard to parse at that age, even when it's neat, heterosexual, socially sanctioned. It's possible that some girls made a shrewd decision to explore in plain sight, through the stealth of irony and tipsiness. For all the regrettable accusations we used to throw around about 'lipstick lesbians', I still believe it was far more common for girls to pretend to be straight than pretend to be gay. I wouldn't judge a young, queer girl for smuggling their true feelings under this shroud. The thought of this song as a site of becoming, however flawed, is comforting.

Though I wouldn't learn of Max Martin's hand in writing this song until years later, I intuited that choices were being made for us about what a girl should be, the 'good' and 'bad' ways she might transgress. This man I've never met has written songs that bookmark every significant point in my coming of age. There he is at six years old and ten years old and twelve and again at twenty-seven, behind my shoulder as I slut drop and finger snap and screech into an imaginary microphone.

Max Martin doesn't look how you'd expect. His face is a strange cross between a comic-book Viking and the lead of a Christian metal band. *I was scared of him.* This is the rumoured reaction Britney had when the two first met. Yet he could walk past most of us in the street and we'd be none the wiser. That's true power: seamless, silent and anonymous. Without the favour of these songwriters, producers, executives, Britney and countless other angel-faced girls like her become Ariel, stranded and voiceless on the shore.

We used to claim allegiance to pop stars. I remember debating for hours with friends over who was better, Christina or Britney. Who you chose said something about you, supposedly. But this feeling of variety and choice was a total illusion. Like Coke and Pepsi made by the same evil corporation, it was the same men writing songs for supposedly 'warring' pop stars, the same companies that moulded them to more or less the same ends, with arbitrary distinctions in styling and targeted demographic.

But, still, I adored pop music. I adored it then and I adore it now. My life has been buoyed and cushioned by its comforting formula, the daisy chain of verse, bridge, chorus. It gave me reliable joy in the shaky years of youth. I no longer berate myself for not having 'better' taste. In my next life, maybe I'll have a more refined cultural palate. I'll listen to German noise bands, Japanese jazz, Icelandic hang drum instrumentals. But on this particular go around the earth I am what I am, namely a whore for the Top 40 hits of the nineties and noughties.

A good pop song is like an old friend in a new hat. As any mathematician knows, a successful formula is as much about the elegant efficiency of the approach as the end result. Pop songs are easy catalysts. As my memories get fainter, the music grows louder: the only thing I can return to and find intact. My memories continually betray me, but music rarely does.

★

I am on my way back from a poetry gig with my friend Hollie. We stop for petrol in Lyme Regis and I wander into a charity shop. A twang of nostalgia pulls me to the CD section. I buy six to listen to on the rest of the journey for the cost of a medium coffee. Not so long ago, I would scrimp and save to buy just one CD. Now they're barely worth the cracked plastic jackets they're in. After several house moves, it became increasingly untenable to drag my CD collection from flat share to flat share. So one year, I gave them all away. But there, like a time capsule from my youth, was a copy of the *...Baby One More Time* album, calling out to me from a charity shop in a tiny seaside town. With my first copy languishing in the stock-room of some other charity shop, or more likely living the rest of its days in landfill, I bought the album for the second time.

It's silly, really. There's an AUX cable in Hollie's car. I pay for a Spotify account on which I can listen to virtually any artist at any time. But I crave a sense of ceremony. I want the cumbersome process of holding the disc at its edges as I feed it into the player. I want to unfold the CD's insert like a map and read along to the lyrics. I want to feel like I did in Auntie E's living room, when access to music was not a given and so it felt like a gift.

The album cover gives me the same feeling as an old holiday photo, warm and peaceful, implacably mournful. What would eight-year-old Vanessa think of me now, holding this copy of something that had once been my most prized possession? Now it's no more than a museum piece, a relic of all that's behind me.

I show my haul of CDs to Hollie, who squints at the cover art for several moments. On the front, Britney stares down the camera lens, her hands clasped exactly as I remembered. On the back is another image of her shot from above. I imagine the cameraman hovering like a storm cloud, how Britney must have craned her neck to look up at the unblinking lens. Her legs are folded awkwardly underneath her, her face tilted and her mouth stretched into a catalogue-grade smile. Her denim skirt is no shorter than what was fashionable to wear for the average teen at the time, but short nonetheless. Between her thighs, a narrow canyon of shadow.

Hollie declares it the point of view of a paedophile. I am taken aback, then taken aback that I'm taken aback. I scrabble to place it into context, that context being no more than: 'It didn't seem that way at the time.' Sometimes it is easier, more soothing, not to look back with the eyes of an adult, to remember things as they seemed when you first saw them.

As miles of motorway disappear behind us, Hollie plays each CD in turn and we sing our throats hoarse. I don't want the car to stop or the song to end – to be left with the angry thud of my thoughts fills me with dread. I know that once Hollie drops me off I'll be left with this grim CD case, with that same fuzzy warmth. What began as a fun throwback is now a reckoning. One of the many costs of growing older is that joy can never be uncomplicated. It is always haunted with the ghosts of grief and regret. I must confess, I gave the CD away to my local charity shop some weeks later. I buried it at the bottom of the plastic bag, underneath some old clothes. I couldn't bear to see Britney staring up at me, cursed to stay sixteen forever.

Despite my hankering for fame, I never went to stage school. At the time, I wasn't aware that institutions for committed show-offs existed, which is probably a blessing in disguise. It meant I had to work with what I had, namely the less than glamorous but perfectly serviceable playground during break time. My only accomplices were the classmates I could successfully wrangle into my vision for an all-girl group. It's my solemn belief that within the break time dance routine are the intricate power dynamics found in every high-powered boardroom and warring nation state. It's a subtle battle of wills and tussle for rank favouring the pretty, agile and, in my case, pathologically bossy.

With the precious thirty minutes between morning and afternoon lessons, I led our 'rehearsals' with a zeal bordering on tyrannical. Though we had no grand performance we were preparing for, we imagined the hungry gaze of a camera lens, a ten-thousand-strong audience. Around us, the other kids screeched their way through their games of catch and Stuck in the Mud, skinning palms and knees, making and betraying promises. None of them looked over at us, except to intercept their filthy footballs that sometimes sailed past our heads.

I assigned myself founder, lead singer and choreographer of the group. We were called The Honey Girlz with a Z, in subtle homage to Sugababes. I liked their name but not their distinctly British nonchalance; my vision for the band lay firmly in the glossy mania of big-budget American pop. The music videos I studied and modelled us on were the end result of hours of professional rehearsal. I gamely sought the same slickness from our hapless quartet of eight-year-olds. They were gormless, their focus splintered and their mouths dusted with Bourbon crumbs. Georgia's fingers were usually gummed with PVA, Jade could barely turn on the spot without getting dizzy and Zia couldn't stop picking at her eczema-speckled skin.

Every count down from five was an act of faith, another chance to get it right. We would stumble upon it, once or twice, the miracle of five unruly bodies falling into sync. These moments of well-oiled synchronicity were such a rush precisely because they were rare. I miss them now, still. I wished so desperately, then, to be taken seriously. Thank god the world kept on, indifferent to our efforts. Thank god fate never called my bluff and made us famous. I doubt we'd have survived it.

★

My singing voice has always been thin. I don't sound awful, just not good. Preferable, I reckon, to be wincingly shit than this. I don't so much hold a note as cling to it. In church services, I mouth the words to the hymns. Karaoke is an abject ritual of torment. Even in the privacy and flattering acoustics of the shower, I don't dare sing. Instead, I thieve the glory of the gifted by miming along to their voices. With all the hard work done for me, I grip an aerosol can and make my bottom lip do its Whitney quiver. I push from my diaphragm and squeeze my eyes shut for the long, belting notes.

I used to listen to Michael deliver the opening croon on 'Who's Lovin' You', finger pre-emptively rested on my Walkman's rewind button. What a way to start a song. I was addicted to that roiling blues chord on the piano, the pleading reach of that beginning riff. I pressed the button so it rolled over and under itself like a tide. The heft of the whole song is contained in those first fifteen seconds, the agonised stretch of that one word: *when*. That truly was the question. When would I get to enjoy the horror of my heart being smashed to pieces by some no-good lover? *Whe-eee-eee-een*. It was longing made audible and tangible. I imitated what I'd seen in movies, tracing raindrops down windows with my fingers, heaving world-weary sighs. It felt good and serious, this theatre of lovesick mourning, like preparation.

Michael was ten years old when the Jackson 5 recorded the song, not much older than I was on that first trip to HMV.

Auntie E had no satisfying answers for why he was so good, so young. Sometimes she said he was anointed. Once, she pondered if he was an alien. His talent was not to be assessed too closely. It defied logic, this divine, galactic thing he had. My job was to marvel from afar.

Now, I am looking. I no longer believe in effortlessness. Talent like Michael's is made in a crucible, beginning with a seed of promise. But these seeds are everywhere, dormant or modestly sprouting in thousands of people. Something set Michael apart, then sent him into the stratosphere. But what? It must have been, in part, the relentless rehearsals, the regular late-night performances on the Chitlin' Circuit, the unforgiving standards of his father whose own dreams of musical stardom never came to fruition. A child isn't guaranteed to become an MJ-level performer if put under the same pressure, but it's hard to conceive of them reaching his level without it.

Describing the early days of singing in his youth, Michael enjoyed the process of watching, mimicking and perfecting. First, he watched and copied his older brothers, quickly surpassing their abilities. He then studied his heroes, stalwart performers like Jackie Wilson and James Brown. He borrowed prolifically, taking the moves and methods of his heroes and metabolising them into something unique. He was unusually precocious. There was a diligence and ambition in him that existed outside his father's firm hand or the fame machine that would soon surround him. In many interviews he describes his perfectionist tendency to work on things obsessively, forever chasing 'more' and 'better'. The line between this and his father's exacting style of management is clear. But his brothers did not become the singular talent that he did, though they were raised by the same man. Michael's determination surpassed his upbringing, spurning the age-old debate of where free will begins and ends. We can never fully trust our own testimony, the self-determining stories we tell about who we are and why.

She's a little show-off, isn't she? Variations of that were said to and about me as a kid. It was true. I was, I am. Funny, as my mother was reserved and thoughtful, never cared to hold court or play jester. I struggle to account for my early appetite for the spotlight. Unlike Michael, I wasn't competing for favour with a gaggle of siblings. Mine was the familiar ballad of the latchkey kid. It was my task to keep myself alive and occupied with as little supervision as possible. I became adept at the elaborate rituals of the solitary. I read a lot and lived inside my headphones. I loved to people-watch and earwig on conversations. My curiosity often tipped into nosiness, the barely disguised voyeurism that probably led to me becoming a writer. And write I did – pages and pages of rambling fantasy stories and earnest rhyming poetry. It was said by relatives and teachers and random strangers alike that I was 'mature for my age'. They said it as if it was a good thing, so I assumed it was.

The praise was addictive. Whatever brought it on, I dialled up. The long words I learnt in my books I dropped into conversation. Even if I misused them, people seemed charmed by my efforts. I learnt the shape of a good joke, the inherent comedy of big hand gestures and an exaggerated pout. Making people laugh was intoxicating. A living room full of adults was the best training ground. Their attention was hard to earn and dazzling to receive. As the uncles sunk can after can of beer and the aunties' shoulders shook with laughter, I would sit in the corner like a favoured pet and absorb the scene as if I'd be asked to recall its details the next day. One uncle let me take gulps from his can of Guinness. I hated its foamy texture and bitter taste, but I took the gulps anyway. They seemed to forget I was there, making seedy jokes and letting meaty bits of family gossip slip. I gained a lot of intel from this decision adults had made about me, that I was 'mature'. It didn't occur to me to think of what they gained in turn, the responsibilities they absolved themselves of.

We talk of old heads on young shoulders. Less is said about the simpler, sadder idea that children learn to cultivate and perfect whatever earns them praise in the absence of unconditional acceptance. The aping of adult-like postures might signal preternatural maturity. More likely, it's a Pavlovian response to what evokes that dangerous facsimile of love: approval.

In *Dead Famous: An Unexpected History of Celebrity from Bronze Age to Silver Screen*, historian Greg Jenner describes how the volatile moods of child actors were managed on film sets in the 1930s. He writes: 'the producers built a soundproof, cramped box in which was stored a large block of ice. This cell was used to punish naughty cast members, with the troublesome toddlers being made to stand in the cold, or even sit directly on the ice, until they'd learned their lesson.'

And what lesson was this? That in that hallowed space of potential fame and riches, they were no longer children. They were products. But since performing is something that so many people enjoy and aspire to, we struggle to see it as work. It seems, conversely, like a wild privilege, to twist and simper in exchange for applause and money.

Michael dodged the worst of his father's beatings partly because he honed his performance skills to such a degree that by the time he was seven he was consistently and undeniably brilliant. Michael's prowess then became the benchmark for the rest of his brothers. *Do it like Michael* was Joe's refrain. The rest of the group would face the wrath of his switch if they didn't meet his exacting standards. Excellence, then, was a survival tactic.

The formula for a compelling child star is evergreen. A cute face (dimples non-essential but preferred). White teeth and wide eyes. We want them brilliant yet unwitting, their quips laced with inadvertent wisdom. A child too aware of their own artifice is a tragic spectacle. We would be confronted with what we have forced on them, the fetishistic edge of our gaze. A child star must somehow walk this tightrope, be partly in on the joke but not entirely. They are entertaining not because of but in spite of themselves.

The child star can also inspire distrust, a disconcerting belief that inside their childlike body is a conniving adult. In his autobiography, *Moonwalk*, Michael recounts how people responded to him in the early days of The Jackson 5. At a talent contest, a member of a rival band referred to him as a 'forty-five-year-old midget'. Decades earlier, Shirley Temple had to fend off rumours that she was 'a thirty-year-old dwarf'. We seem to want both fantasies simultaneously, that of the naturally charming child and the wily adult masquerading as one. Perhaps this reconciles our unease with these prodigies and their uncanny talent. Like Auntie E insisted, the rules that applied to the rest of us did not apply to them. They were angels or aliens, maybe even monsters. But they were something other than human, a fact for which they'd be praised and punished.

Auntie E had the *Dangerous* music videos on VHS and I loved the behind-the-scenes footage as much as the videos themselves. I remember the outtakes from the 'Black Or White' video the best. Michael had a large group of kids with him on set, including *Home Alone* star Macaulay Culkin, and they all ran riot in the studio. They chased each other in manic circles, shooting jets of water out of toy guns and hurling cream pies at each other's faces. Watching made my chest ache. I wanted to be with them. It's a scene of idyllic childhood on steroids, something an eight-year-old might draw when given the prompt 'My Perfect Day'.

Now I know that candour can be engineered. But we can know these things yet still respond to their emotive ploys. Even when I rewatch the scenes now, I struggle to lay a veil of cynicism over the scene. Long before social media birthed the acronym FOMO to describe this feeling, I used to sit in front of the TV and wish I was somewhere else and someone other than who I was. I wanted the impossible: to live in a curated fiction, a retroactive fairy tale. I wanted to live in a neverland.

In 2019, the *Leaving Neverland* documentary came out. My algorithm kept suggesting it to me, the thumbnail hovering like a threat. When people asked if I'd watched it, I'd say no, not yet. The truth was I had no intention to. Sure, I had shared social media posts that insisted We Must Believe Victims. And I did, almost always. What I felt wasn't outright denial. That, at least, would have been less discomfiting. It was more like the dread of sitting in a dentist's waiting room, telling myself I could walk out at any moment. I knew that documentary would hurt, that a line of knowing would be crossed that I couldn't walk back.

Eventually, my weakness embarrassed me. What exactly was I protecting? By then, Michael had been dead for ten years. My obsession was also dead, leaving only the faintest ghost of fondness. I'd begun to nurse the quiet belief that what they said about Michael might be true. In all other instances, I would never dismiss anyone's claims of abuse, not because no one ever lies about these things but because it's so rare that they do. This felt firm, true and incontestable. Yet when it came to Michael, my resolve took its leave.

But I made myself watch it, in the end. It was the crushing experience I had feared. But there was something else, too. An odd flush of relief. I could finally stop lying to myself. I could stop protecting Michael the figure, the demigod, and begin to see him as the fallible human he was. I felt deeply foolish, yet it was a clarifying moment. I was standing at the edge of my morality, observing its limits and brittle foundations.

Those poor boys, now men, sitting there reliving the awful things that had happened, eyes steady to the camera. I couldn't, cannot imagine, would never deign to try. How remarkable that they could sit there and speak plainly, name what was done and how. And I had refused to engage all this time, for what? So that I might listen to my precious pop songs guilt free. So my fantasy of who Michael was could not be overwritten by the hideous reality of what he did and the lives he ruptured.

Of all the revelations from the documentary, I was most haunted by the testimony from Wade Robson's mother, Joy. She had a warm and slightly wizened face framed by a sweep of orangey red hair with a white streak at the front. She was alone and well-lit, in an armchair pushed against a wall. Sometimes the camera films her from above. We quite literally look down at her as she describes repeatedly leaving her son alone with Michael, eventually moving her entire family from Australia to the US to be closer to him.

Recollecting the early days of Michael's interest in her son, Joy's face lights up. She was dazzled by his rapport with Wade, the phone calls and lavish gifts, the personal invite to the Neverland Ranch. 'I think I've died and gone to heaven,' she said to herself as she surveyed the lavish grounds, and her eyes glitter as she recalls the memory. She's enthralled, still, even in light of all that transpired. Her obliviousness is hard to reckon with and even harder not to judge. How could she not know, or even suspect, what was happening?

The court of Reddit hasn't much sympathy for Joy. In florid paragraphs, these courtroom jurors call her everything from a gold digger to a full-blown psychopath. Some even accuse her of being a co-conspirator in her son's abuse. I feel the urge to defend her, not because I know them to be wrong but because a part of me fears that, in her position, I may have behaved the same. She is a magpie like me. I, too, have dyed my hair traffic-light bright, been drawn to the fool's gold of status and fame.

Something about Michael eroded her questioning mind. In his presence, she was willing and gullible. Listening to his music rewinds time, like the brown tape wound back into its cassette. Press play and I'm a kid again, all eyes and awe and wonder. I recognise Joy's dilemma, her words still marred by the stubborn residue of worship.

It was heartbreak watching that documentary, letting Michael topple from his golden perch in my mind. He had taken my faith in my own judgement, my own eyes. I am aware of how hyperbolic this sounds. But this is how it felt. I am aware, also, how bizarre it is to personalise a tragedy that didn't even happen to me. But this is how it felt. Whether or not my feelings were justified or proportional, there they were.

First, there was a brief, gratifying spurt of rage. How dare he not be what he claimed, what I insisted he be! That felt good and urgent, like anger often does. It felt like I was doing something, Then, I considered myself, my hollow atheist posturing, how I claimed not to follow any deity yet still sought the comfort of an external power. This was what Michael was for Joy. A mentor for her talented child, a quasi-parental figure. Michael's interest was affirmation that Wade, and by extension she, was special. This bludgeoned Joy's discernment, with disastrous consequences. At Neverland, there was no space for fear or scepticism. It was the flattened 'heaven' of a child's imagination, unsullied by time or responsibility.

Michael described the Neverland Ranch as the world of play and freedom he never got to experience as a child. But what child has a personal zoo in their backyard, a home cinema, round-the-clock staff at their beck and call? Neverland is the idyllic childhood that none of us get to have. Even the most untroubled childhood is pockmarked by disillusion, necessary glimpses into the world's cruelty. Michael's childhood was marred by both the common scourge of abuse and the unusual spectre of fame. The result seems to be two major distortions.

One, that a fantasy of childhood might exist, and that he could create and live in it. Two, that his childhood wounds made him incapable of inflicting pain on other people.

It's hard to know how much he believed in the story he told himself about Neverland. Perhaps his insistence that he looked at life through the eyes of a child was always a strategy to lure impressionable children and their willing parents into his orbit. I find it more probable that he actually believed himself a boy stuck in a man's body. Michael as Machiavellian puppet master is not implausible, but this theory is easier to swallow than a more complicated truth. Michael spun a narrative of himself as a guileless child at the mercy of a cruel father and rapacious media. This is part of the story, but not all of it. It's the danger of fairy tales and their familiar shapes, the seductive lull of the senses as we hear the refrain we so desperately crave.

Once upon a time . . .

Track 2: Spinning Tales

Sometimes, though not often, he had dreams, and they were more painful than the dreams of other boys. For hours he could not be separated from these dreams, though he wailed piteously in them. They had to do, I think, with the riddle of his existence.

—J. M. Barrie

Little-known fact: Michael was set to play Peter Pan in a feature film directed by Steven Spielberg. This was in the late eighties when Michael's quirks were still seen as amusing rather than sinister. The movie never got made in the end, but I like to conjure my own montage of what could have been. Michael in a bright green smock chasing after animated pirates, sat on a windowsill singing a duet with a Tinkerbell voiced by Barbra Streisand or Liza Minnelli.

Throughout his career, Michael expressed deep affinity with the character. At Neverland, Michael kept several pieces of Peter Pan memorabilia, including a bronze Peter Pan statue on the grounds. It was an identification that reified itself, the sort of repeated insistence you see from a child newly obsessed with this or that toy or topic. Note that Peter Pan is The Boy Who *Wouldn't* Grow Up. It is a rigid, inflexible statement. Michael's was not an involuntary condition: it was a choice. Peter Pan, bestowed with a rare gift that makes him compelling to everyone around him, is nonetheless tortured by his difference. In this light, Michael's affinity with him feels less silly and more devastating.

Staying young forever sounds fun in theory, but in the story Peter is forced to watch as his friend Wendy grows older, gets married, bears her own children and eventually dies, all while he remains frozen in time. He is both obsessed with and resentful of Wendy, his constant reminder that his stubborn worldview isolates him from everyone else around him. The story of Peter Pan explores the irresolvable loss that comes with growing up. Perpetual childhood preserves the possibility of the future without having to actually arrive at it. If time doesn't move forward, there is no need for reckoning, no reaping of hastily sown seeds. In light of what Michael did, it makes grim sense why this idea might have appealed to him.

Robson described how a Peter Pan poster on Michael's bedroom wall kept watch over them as the sexual abuse unfurled.

Before their friendship turned physical, their hangouts were like playdates between kids of a similar age. They played video games and visited toy stores, watched just-released movies in Michael's home cinema. Neverland was Michael's Peter Pan syndrome made physical, a fortress of plausible denial built to attract children. In Neverland, the indignities of time did not apply. Michael was a Big Kid.

Even so, his body betrayed him. He grew older. The story of himself as encumbered by the body and life of a grown man began to lose its eccentric charm. But the more apparent this became, the more he seemed to double down. His was a hideous trap of innocence deferred and adulthood made weapon. Like many of the young boys Michael kept company with, Robson describes being with Michael like playing with a fellow child. This is one of many subtle cruelties in how such abuse unfolds. Namely, the performance of shared innocence and the framing of coercive, adult behaviour as mutually tentative discovery. It's a grim but common reality of sexual abuse that a child, through no fault of their own, might process these adult acts as play and discovery, one of many new things they are introduced to in an infinitely surprising world. With no language or context to frame any unease, the adult who frames these acts as 'love' sets a warped foundation for the child who knows no different. Michael's performance of innocence became both the foil and the propeller of the abuse.

The story of Peter Pan also touches on our neutered idea of what goes on in children's heads. Inevitably, we misremember what it was to be young once we've passed a certain age threshold. As we become the custodians, we aim to preserve an assumed innocence that we wish for our children. But this insistence that children's interior lives are nothing but unicorns and candyfloss is deeply misguided. Peter Pan is not visible to Wendy's mother, and any mention of him is hastily dismissed. It would be unsettling, of course, to hear your young daughter talk of a winged, mischievous boy that regularly visits in the night. But instead of being curious about this, Wendy's mother busies herself with denial. This extract from the book *Peter Pan and Wendy* feels especially apt:

> It is the nightly custom of every good mother after her children are asleep to rummage in their minds and put things straight for next morning, repacking into their proper places the many articles that have wandered during the day . . . When you wake in the morning, the naughtiness and evil passions with which you went to bed have been folded up small and placed at the bottom of your mind and on the top, beautifully aired, are spread out your prettier thoughts, ready for you to put on.

Anything pertaining to the earthly pleasures of the flesh was frowned upon in my house. Sexual frankness, I deduced, was for the ethnically white and spiritually wayward. The very idea that sex logically accounted for my existence was unmentionable. But my mother's disapproval only spurred my curiosity. I gathered intel on what sparked these shocks of carnal electricity: certain words on pages, the liquid black gap between parted lips just before two people kissed on TV, the way the curly hair of certain men fell down their foreheads. If it had some funk of the feral or horny on it, I wanted to know about it. We don't like to think of this, the burgeoning sexuality of children. But it is as true, as real, as any adult's.

When Wendy's mother denies the presence of Peter, she also denies all the unwieldy aspects of herself. Her own deviance and sexuality, her dark thoughts and deep regrets. The things we cannot address for ourselves then become the pathologies we hand down to the children in our care. Later in the book, Wendy's mother finally sees Peter for herself one night as he climbs into her daughter's bedroom window. Briefly, she sees the world through her daughter's eyes and is wiser for it.

For what it's worth, I think Michael is more like Captain Hook than Peter Pan. He is presented as the antagonist but as is often the way, the original book paints a far more nuanced character than most popular versions of the story do. Peter Pan not only cuts off Captain Hook's hand at the top of the story, but he then feeds that hand to a crocodile who chases after Hook hoping to eat the rest of him. Inside that crocodile's stomach is also a clock. Hook becomes callous and vengeful, but who wouldn't be in his position? He is doomed to chase after the unrepentant boy who handicapped him. No one and nothing is on his side, least of all time. Always, his ears are pricked for the sound of ticking.

Interlude #2 – The Audition

A young girl sits in the back of a fancy car, her skinny legs stretched out. If she tried this in her dad's crappy hatchback, the front seat would press into her knees. She doesn't know what make of car this is, only that perched on top of its shiny black hood is a figurine of a winged woman in flight. She looks like an angel, like Tinkerbell from her favourite movie as a kid. This feels like a good sign.

There is a mini-fridge in the car. It is full of small bottles of Coca-Cola stacked neat as a shop display. *Go on, they're for you*, the driver says. She drinks too fast, the fizz making her nostrils flare. The air conditioning is strong and silent. She shivers in her cropped tank top and shorts.

She wonders if he'll look like he does in the poster on her wall. She likes his leather waistcoat and neat cornrows, the fullness of his lips. He probably has a girlfriend or even a wife. But, still, she likes to fantasise about kissing him, what her name would sound like in his voice.

She is fourteen but looks older depending on how she does her hair and make-up. By twelve, she had learnt how to line her lips with a dark brown pencil and fill them in with shimmery gloss. She is pretty. She knows this because family, friends and perfect strangers tell her so. Once, a grown man nearly got himself run over dashing across the street to holler at her.

The girl's name is Angie, after a dead grandmother she only knows from photos. She is told she has her big eyes, her sweet singing voice. Angie's nana had her mama at sixteen and Angie's mama had her at seventeen. Where she lives, most girls her age can cook, clean and cuss as good as anyone. It's no thing to have a boyfriend in college or working clippers at a barbershop, maybe even a desk job. Get you a man that's grown and paid, her big sister always says. Guys her age were scrubs and chancers anyway, type to make you split a shake on a date then run out on the bill.

Angie's heart beats slow and thick. All she has to do is sing her song.

They have been driving for what feels like hours. She doesn't recognise the streets they're passing.

Under her breath she recites a string of numbers. Learning it off by heart was the condition of being able to go, since her mother couldn't take a day off work to come with her.

Call me as soon as you get there, okay? Don't be a nuisance. And you're to address him as Mr Kelly, understand?

The driver keeps asking her questions. If she's comfortable, if the temperature's okay, what church she sings at. He catches her eye in the rearview mirror, the hint of a question in the arch of his brows. He says he has a daughter the same age as her, his pride and joy. She smiles tightly in response, stares out of the tinted window.

As the car pulls slowly to a stop at what she assumes is the house, she drinks the rest of her soda in one hasty gulp, her mouth filling with sweet froth.

The driver gets out of the car and walks to her side to open the door. Years later, when she tries to remember the details of this first introduction (the journalist placed a dirty glass of water and a box of tissues between them, the questions kept coming and coming and coming), she'll struggle to recall the colour of the front door, whether there were or weren't palm trees along the drive, if he shook her hand or hugged her the first time they met. She does remember how he shook his head when she greeted him as her mother had instructed. *Please, call me Robert.* He'd seemed kind of nervous, which made her feel more comfortable. His large hands folded in and out of his pockets. Even his laughter sounded like singing.

The driver had stopped her just before they walked into the

house, leant down to whisper in her ear. *Does your father know you're here?*

She showed the driver the R. Kelly cassette in her bag, told him her dad was a big fan. He'd made her promise to bring the tape back signed.

> *Once more he stept into the street;*
> *And to his lips again*
> *Laid his long pipe of smooth straight cane;*
> . . .
> *Small feet were pattering, wooden shoes clattering,*
> *Little hands clapping, and little tongues chattering,*
> *And, like fowls in a farm-yard when barley is scattering,*
> *Out came the children running.*
>
> —Robert Browning

The playlist at a typical Ugandan wedding is a strange and endearing artefact. On there, you will definitely find some Michael and also some Celine Dion or Shakira, the elevator jazz of Kenny G (I cannot account for or defend my people, I am simply stating the facts as they stand). Ugandans also love a bit of R. Kelly. One song guaranteed to get everyone off their plastic seats and onto the dance floor is 'Happy People'. It's one of those diasporic super-tunes, a song just as likely to get the crowd going in Atlanta as Peckham or Lagos as Kingston. It has the nostalgic, feelgood groove of songs from the seventies and eighties, makes you hanker, vaguely, for the 'good old days' even if you're too young to have any to look back to. It's a cheesy song, lolloping and long. I love it. My mother does, too. Never one to make an exhibition of herself, she is content to sit on the side and bob her head to the rhythm. It's her own form of letting loose, like those tapping fingers on the steering wheel. We have sat many times and listened to that song in her living room. Increasingly, listening to R. Kelly's music feels untenable for me. But I haven't the heart to tell my mother to stop playing the song. It would be one less shared thing, another string of connection severed.

Like his musical hero Michael Jackson, R. Kelly used a mythical figure in his personal branding to great effect. He named himself 'The Pied Piper of R&B', often quoting this moniker at the beginning of his songs. It was a genius bit of shorthand, signalling that R. Kelly's music drew large crowds and loyal fans.

Until recently, my grasp on the Pied Piper story didn't go much further than the image of a sprightly man with a humble pipe, a trail of music-drunk children in his wake. But just like Peter Pan, the Pied Piper is a more complicated character than his popular depiction suggests. Admittedly, the tale begins with a rather unsexy inciting incident: the struggles of vermin control. The Pied Piper is hired by the mayor of a small village to entice a scourge of rats away from the streets and to drown them in the river. The piper does this with ease, much to the delight of the villagers.

But the story doesn't end there. When the piper doesn't receive the payment he was promised, he wreaks his revenge by playing his pipe again, this time to entice all of the village's children to follow him. And so the ominous parallels with the Pied Piper and R. Kelly continue. The latter made a habit of grooming young girls and women, often with promises of musical success.

Nothing illustrates this better than the album cover for Aaliyah's debut album *Age Ain't Nothing But A Number.* She poses on the left of the shot, the epitome of nineties tomboy cool. Behind her, blurred but still visible, is the hunched figure of a man on the phone. He looks over his shoulder at her. It's the paranoid stance of a bodyguard or jealous boyfriend. The man in the picture is R. Kelly, who had huge input on Aaliyah's vocal stylings, lyrics and clothing. He also wrote the titular single for the album, an R&B slow jam written from the perspective of a young woman seducing an older man.

We now know that once R. Kelly had built trust with the girls he groomed, he would begin a campaign of control, dictating what they wore and ate, who they could speak to and even when they could use the toilet. Distressed parents reported not hearing from their children for years. But, continually, it was insisted that these girls and women were choosing to be there. Just as the Pied Piper played his pipe and the children 'chose' to follow, it was argued that these girls came of their own volition and could leave with it, too. R. Kelly also learnt to be strategic, making sure the girls he targeted were just over the age of consent. In the eyes of the law, at least, they were adults. R. Kelly was blinded by his rapacious narcissism, committed to the lies he told himself and the myriad of women he abused. But crimes like his do not happen at the scale they do without accomplices and yes men, a pervasive culture of least resistance.

Endings of the Pied Piper story vary. In one, the children all follow the piper into a cave in which they disappear, never to be seen again. In another, all the children but two meet the same fate as the rats by drowning in the river. The pair left behind are disabled: a deaf child who could not hear the piper's music and a crippled child who could not keep pace with everyone else. They report back to the village about the missing children, who are never found and assumed to be dead.

The conclusion of the story skips ahead several years to the discovery of a strange tribe of people residing in Transylvania whose 'outlandish ways and dress' alarm their neighbours. They are rumoured to be the ancestors of an errant group of people from Hamelin who emerged from a 'subterranean prison'. It's a haunting ending, somehow worse than if the children had perished. Instead, they are forced to live in exile, robbed of anything resembling a normal life.

Michael wrote for the ear of a child, favouring melodies that, in his words, 'a five-year-old can sing along to'. His sonic influences spanned pop, gospel, rock, hip hop, R&B, show tunes and classical music. A harsh critic might read this as the net of an opportunist cast indiscriminately wide. But I see this as a continuation of the 'borderless' music Motown made in its prime, pushing past the ghettoising of music and reaching for broad appeal. Cynical reasons for this approach aside, I love the wide appeal of these songs, how they can briefly unite otherwise starkly different people, if only for the duration of a three-minute tune.

I would like to make the case that Michael Jackson was the last truly global currency. A documentary made by film director Erling Söderström illustrates this perfectly. In it, a group of indigenous tribespeople living in the Amazon are shown video footage of major news events: the moon landing, the 9/11 attacks, a major soccer star and, finally, Michael Jackson performing onstage during his *HIStory* World Tour.

Söderström observed: 'They didn't know about the moon landing and were concerned about the negative impact it could have for conditions on Earth. They couldn't understand modern warfare and appeared to be shocked by the footage of the 9/11 attacks in New York. Neither did they know France's most famous soccer star of the day. However, all the young members of the tribe were familiar with Michael Jackson.' This level of ubiquity, pre-internet, is astonishing. As the Ghanaian-American musician Amaarae once quipped on Twitter: 'After Jesus, Michael Jackson is probably the most famous human being to ever exist.'

Michael appealed to the child in many of us, in large part because it's his voice threaded through our formative years, his dance moves that so many of us first tried on for size. He clearly retained some aspect of that wide-eyed, universalist worldview that most of us struggle to hold on to.

There are very few Michael Jackson songs I actively dislike. Even objectively terrible ballads like 'Gone Too Soon' or 'Heal The World' have their furtive place in my heart. I grew fond of these songs through an acclimation that's hard to replicate in our age of streaming. My listening experience used to be limited to the music my family physically owned. Albums needed to be worn in like leather shoes. Other than already released singles, you had no idea what you were getting when buying one. That gamble was part of the thrill. Through repeated listens, you found a way to commune with the music you'd been dealt. Songs that you loved immediately sometimes lost their lustre, while others that initially seemed dull or unlistenable could grow on you with a little patience.

This never happened with 'You Are Not Alone', a love song so cloying it makes my head feel like it's slowly being filled with tapioca pudding. It sucks so bad. It makes Dido sound like System of a Down. The worst of its sins is that it doesn't commit! Schmaltz can always be redeemed by its own excess, but there is none to be found here. The song limps into its key change at the final third, with none of the bombast it so desperately needs. Not even the gospel choir at the end can rescue things. Instead they sound distant and distracted, like they're thinking about their pending lunch break.

Still, the song was a huge success, the last number one Michael would have in the charts before his death. It was written for him by R. Kelly with the songwriting formula he used for his own Sunday-school friendly hits like 'I Believe I Can Fly' and 'The World's Greatest'. These songs evoke the feeling of watching kids' TV with my godson. The twee melodies of these shows lull me into a soporific state, my brain softening like cooked fruit. The melodies of children's ditties and globally popular songs share a loose lineage. Both can soothe and placate, slowly reduce our critical faculties over time. These songs are so pleasing because we know what to expect of them. They do not demand our focus or vigilance. We trust the songs and, by extension and occasionally to our peril, their singers.

A cursory look at R. Kelly's biography reveals a litany of early-life horrors. An absent father, a childhood friend who drowned at the age of eight as he stood by, helpless. Several family members sexually abused him and his brother as children. He struggled academically, his dyslexia so pronounced that he would progress well into adulthood without being able to read or write.

I can't help but wonder what his talent for singing came to represent for him, how his subsequent pursuit of fame may have been warped by these early life experiences. Watching the body of his friend float downstream, he perhaps realised that tragedy is sudden and arbitrary. When an older girl exposed him to her sexual advances, he perhaps absorbed the idea that sex is not an exchange between equals but a battle of wills. In the face of this, fame and the influence it afforded him may have been a deeply twisted attempt to wrest back control.

Though child sexual abuse has all manner of adverse effects on its victims, it must be stressed that most people who experience childhood abuse don't go on to perpetrate it themselves. In a paper published by the Cambridge University Press in 2018, it was stated that although the link between childhood abuse and later predatory behaviour has long been presumed in psychiatric circles, there is not enough empirical evidence to support this theory. That said, though it is not inevitable, it is sadly not exceptional.

Please understand: I am not looking to excuse or minimise. I am trying to grasp what formative abuse can do to a mind that is still cobbling itself together. It takes a certain hubris, perhaps, to do this from a place of philosophical speculation and not expertise, but I have to believe there is use in applying my fledgling heart and intellect to this as a thinker and writer and citizen of the world. Qualification is surely not just about institutionalised permission, but also who has a stake in the issue and that's each and every one of us. A dizzying myriad factors can come together to form a distorted and antisocial script for human relating. Add fame to the mix and we can imagine how tricky it is for a person to see themselves and their impact with clear eyes. It is as if the famous person lives in a claustrophobic hall of mirrors, enamoured with all these distorted, ego-fuelled versions of themselves. It's the bald reality of who they are outside this that becomes intolerable.

We have a paucity of alarm when it comes to the abuse of young boys at the hands of adult women. Of course, we know that, statistically, men commit abuse against people of all genders far more than women do. But this doesn't mean we need not examine the nuance of this less common scenario. I believe our attitudes around this are fed by a few enduring fallacies. We assume that all women are instinctually nurturing, rendering the awareness of female predators negligible or nonexistent. Equally stubborn is the assumed sexual readiness of boys and men. That a boy might feel sexually intimidated or pressured is incongruent with the images we're fed of insatiably horny boys willing to stick their dicks in anything and anyone. The message I received from cultural touchstones like *The Inbetweeners* and *American Pie*, and jokes that boys themselves made, was that sex was welcome no matter the circumstance.

Even when we reject these bioessentialist notions intellectually, they still affect our felt experience of the world. The thought of a young boy being sexually coerced by an older women does not provoke the same instinctual sense of horror in me as the reversed situation does. This is not to say that the thought does not deeply upset and disturb me. It does. It is more a matter of gradation and intensity, the subtle but marked difference in how the feeling sits in my stomach. Simply put, my primordial urge to protect the young girl feels more urgent than it does for the young boy. Believe me, owning this brings me no small amount of shame, but I do so in the hope we might excavate this lopsided thinking together.

I think it's important for us to own this uneven attitude that I suspect many of us have, not because I necessarily think we can shift this gut response completely, but so we can get ahead of our conditioning and question this unequal distribution of empathy. This also goes for male survivors themselves, who often internalise a twisted understanding of the abuse they suffer. It's not uncommon for boys to interpret abuse from older women as consensual. They might even boast about their early sexual experiences with older women, framing them as a badge of honour and virility.

It's always bored and disappointed me that a lot of men's impetus to take feminism seriously comes when they have daughters of their own. But I am forced to say, in a pained stage whisper, that maybe I've been too quick to judge. I now understand how seismic it is when a young, impressionable human is in your care, how it stretches your imagination and forces you out of your long-fixed thoughts and self-serving world view. I have a gorgeous, squishy godson now, and he is making me think anew about the plight of boys. I don't want any natural sexual curiosity he may have to be exploited, or for him to believe that boys always want it and girls must always be convinced. I want better for him than what we had.

Sadly, some people are exposed to sexually inappropriate behaviour at a young age go on to exhibit unhealthy sexual behaviour as adults. As mentioned, this is not an inevitability but a strong indicator, a risk factor we must take seriously if we want to address this issue at its root. What children learn about intimacy, not just from what they're told, but what they're modelled by others around them, is crucial.

Unless he instructs us otherwise, my godson will move through this world socialised as a boy with all the benefits and costs that entails. The dangers of how we silo the different genders goes deeper than the choice to dress them in pink or blue. Where we place them on the axis of vulnerability is also compromised. The stories we tell boys about their bodies and the value others inscribe upon them will form not just what they believe others have a right to do to them, but what they can do to others in turn. The children we love should grow up knowing that entitlement and compassion cannot co-exist. Their bodies are their own, and the care they wish others to have for theirs must be extended to everyone else's.

The older I get, the more untethered I become from my body. With my godson, I am slammed back into myself. The joy of it never fails to throw me into pre-emptive mourning for when he grows older and out of himself. So much is coming for him. But no matter. Right now, he is proto-dancing. He throws his fists out, two glorious bombs of dimpled chub, and YELPS. He wriggles to the beat, which I imagine climbing up his spine like mercury through a thermometer. He is drowning in his own giggles, a pendulum of saliva swinging from his mouth. I feel it with him, how physical life is, its every jolt and shiver.

Here, in the indelible contract of the printed word, I make him a promise. I will not dismiss the fruits of his wonderful mind. I will use my imagination to create ways to protect him that don't diminish his right to choose his own life and his own mistakes.

When he crawls along the floor, exploring the contours of a room both familiar and endlessly novel, I see the simultaneity of the space as if through his eyes. On one hand, it is the comfortable living room that he spends every day in. On the other, it is an endless menu of potential hazards. The wooden floors, the candles in their glass cylinders, the corners of bookshelves and coffee tables: all threaten to damage his precious little body. But I do not stop him exploring. He must learn by doing and feeling and, yes, sometimes hurting.

They say we get to see the world through a child's eyes again through parenthood. I've had a wonderful glimpse of this through hanging out with G, but I don't think I'll have my own children for a multitude of reasons. One of them is the unsolvable conundrum of what on earth you're supposed to tell a child about this beautiful and hideous world. How might I explain how things work around here? Every time I think I have a handle on it, I am knocked by a wave of my own arrogance or ignorance. I have no idea what's going on. Who am I to try and guide a child through a maze I don't know my way out of?

All too soon, a child sees a news bulletin about another senseless war, watches one kid push another in the playground. They will see the myriad hypocrisies of their parents and seethe.

I imagine my godson at three, five and eight years old, and all the questions he might ask me. Who decided the names for all the colours? Why can't human beings fly? Where do dead people live? Why do human beings hurt each other?

For all my scepticism about the giving of advice, I like the idea of having at least *some* answers. Is that a gift I can bestow to a child? Something steady, something like certainty? I suppose this is what my mother tried to give me by raising me Christian. For a long time, I saw this as indoctrination, but now I appreciate the gift it was, though I found no long-term use for it. It was a sincere attempt to offer me something solid in a tumultuous world, a god whom I might visit when the world feels especially senseless. It is what they gave me, by accident, with Michael. But both these figures failed me, in the end. I won't pretend I don't miss the tethered feeling they gave me, that borrowed but no less blissful sense of purpose.

G might also turn to the false idols that too many of us favour. So I make the only promise I think I am able to keep: that I will sit with his questions and not insult him with easy answers. I will believe in the world as he describes it to me, in all its improbable vigour and vividness, even if I can't access it. Especially if I can't access it. In a notebook, I write him a note for the future. It reads:

Oh, you brief miracle of a boy. How tall you have grown, how impossible to measure.

Do you remember the song I sang for you as a baby? My-call, my-call.

I know I said you can ask me anything but don't ask me about that. About him.

Neverland

He is/was my hero.
Don't have one of those,
if you can help it.

(So few of us can.
So very few of us can.)

MAGIC

My cousin Clive and I are sat cross-legged on the dusty floor of the hall. We are comparing tongues. Mine is Panda Pops blue and his is the red of glacé cherries and fake blood. '1er Gaou' belches from the speakers and the dancefloor in front of us is filling up. Through the forest of adult legs I see knee-height kids dancing, flashes of taffeta, the big heads of loud boys bobbing. The soapy liquid in my bubble tube has almost run out. I hold the wand in front of my mouth and blow one last time, beguiled by the rainbows on each bubble's skin. Uncle E is in the corner of the room, can of Guinness in hand. He pats his open mouth to make an ululating sound. All the other uncles join in, sounding like a chorus of car alarms.

Clive points to the black scuffs on my white tights. *You're gonna get slapped for that*, he says, pulling chicken off a drumstick with his brace-rimmed teeth. The roof of my mouth is coated in syrup-thick saliva, and I am too addled with sugar to care about any pending punishment. I am twitchy with the thrill of everyone in their shiny outfits, the coloured lights that kaleidoscope across our faces. I have too few limbs for all the energy in my body.

Clive pokes my shoulder with his picked-clean chicken bone,

grins a greasy grin: *Bet you can't beat me in a dance competition.* He thinks he's got it in the bag because he's three years older and several inches taller. But I've been practising precisely for moments like this. We find a corner of the floor, the younger kids circling us. Sisqó's 'Thong Song' is playing and the adults glance over, sensing that we might provide some entertainment. They throw their weight into proceedings, hedging bets on who will win. Uncle E pulls a five-pound note out of his wallet and waves it in front of us, promising it to whoever dances the best.

The thought of losing to Clive makes the swirl of undigested gateau in my stomach rise back up my throat. We go at it, me whirling and cocking my leg, him a manic, pop-locking robot. The room is a shaken snowglobe of lights, colour, shouts. As the song builds to its climax, I cannot move my body fast enough. My chest is a slowly filling balloon about to burst. Then, just as Sisqó lets out his final, primal yell, Clive does it: a flawless moonwalk spanning one end of the floor to the other. He full-stops it with a crotch grab, a perfectly timed flick of his jacket. It is done. The response from everyone is so thunderous that Uncle pulls his wallet from his back pocket and swaps the five-pound note for a tenner. Clive does a victory dance as everyone circles him, clapping and cheering his name. I feel a squeeze on my shoulder. It is Uncle, giving me a look that soothes the sting a little. It was the second magic trick I saw and eventually mastered. Silence could morph into applause, art into money.

The next day, I am still sore from the loss. The afternoon took forever to arrive, but it came, and with it an ice cream van drives slowly down the street, playing its tinkly waltz. Uncle

E gives me a pound coin and off I run. That small piece of metal would then transform itself into a Mr Whippy cone with a fat chocolate flake, a drizzle of strawberry sauce for no extra charge as the ice cream man was in a good mood. What was this equation, this alchemy, which turned a coin into an ice cream, a fat paper bag of fizzy cola bottles, a bus journey into town?

Many times, I've tried and failed to get my head around economics. I scan the theories and squint at the graphs. I read and re-read the definitions of compound interest and liquid assets, comb through all the acronyms. The more I read, the less sense any of it makes. Economics is not a science, but economists discuss it as if it were. To me, the subject of money feels deeply steeped in mysticism. Everything from the slippery, obfuscating language we use to talk about it to the untethered worth of money itself feels like a dark art.

But as a kid, I didn't know or care how money worked. I just knew I loved the reassuring feeling of a coin tucked into my palm, the comforting, musty smell it left on my fingers. Even the dirty, citric tang of a coin when I pressed it to my tongue pleased me. The best of the ice cream buying was just before the having, the reaching up and out for the cone, the top of my head only just reaching the van's hatch. The thrilling horror of seeing up the ice cream man's nostrils, the cone's perfect turret of cream pointing to the sky. I plant the coin in the flat meat of his hand. He closes his fingers around it, and the moment is gone. I eat the ice cream in breathless gasps so it doesn't slide onto the floor or drip down my arm in the afternoon heat.

* * *

As anyone who's had a coin 'magically' found behind their ear will know, money is an essential tool in a magician's repertoire. Coins are especially good for tricks. They are small and portable, easy to get and manipulate. They can be double-headed or foldable and are seemingly familiar at a glance. A coin represents the story of money, which is the story of human endeavour, the movements of tribes, the drive to make and sustain a home.

An uneasy marriage exists between money and magical thinking. We see evidence of this in the ritualistic behaviours on game shows like *Deal or No Deal*, where a game of pure chance is reframed as a test of intuition and self-belief. The best-selling self-help book *The Secret* encourages its readers to think of money like a pesky yet highly suggestible lover. Money can, its author Rhonda Byrne claims, be willed into being through the power of positive thought alone. A preposterously elegant concept: poor people have no money simply because *they don't want it enough*. At the behest of charismatic church leaders, loyal congregants donate money they can scarcely afford to give away in deference to the so-called 'prosperity gospel', a promise of riches in a distant future, or promised afterlife, even in the face of present hardship. Many of us, consciously or not, see money as both a solemn, earthly resource and a magic token.

It became apparent that if I wanted money, I had to appease and charm the adults around me to get it. Uncle seemed to have infinite amounts of it. He always kept a folded wad of cash in a money clip, and was always keen to show me some new watch or pair of shoes he'd bought from Harrods. He wasn't like Auntie, who always squinted at the cost of items in the supermarket, picking things up only to put them down. If I wanted a trip to Pizza Hut, Uncle was most likely to cave, to let me order the Happy Meal *and* the McFlurry, a vanilla milkshake I could never finish.

Only later would Auntie tell me about the debt and missed rent payments, the money that was supposed to be for bills that transformed into ostentatious gift boxes. He would leave them on the bed for her to find before he disappeared to the pub. I imagined her lifting the lid, dreading what she'd find under the tissue paper. Inside would be clothes for her younger self. Negligees meant for a figure she hadn't had in years, patent leather heels a size too small. Uncle E gone, without so much as a finger click or puff of smoke.

The Magic Trick of Money and Memory

The moonwalk is the first magic trick I ever witnessed and the first I attempted. For many years, any smooth floor was an opportunity to perfect the impossible. Things I noted over many failed tries: cheap vinyl floors were superior to wooden ones. It was easier to do in socks, but this was a placeholder, like riding a bike with stabilisers.

Auntie E's long, narrow kitchen was ideal to practise in. It had a doorless entrance and the shiny lino was chequered like a chess board. I liked to fit my feet neatly inside one of the white squares, imagine my foot had caused it to glow like in the 'Billie Jean' video. There was a clear sightline from the living room to the kitchen, and from the right angle I could usually see Auntie and Uncle on the sofa watching telly. Back and forth I slid across the floor. From the doorway's frame, Uncle and Auntie would appear and disappear, awash in a ghostly blue glow. Sometimes Uncle would spot me and wink, like we shared a secret.

In the 'Billie Jean' video, Michael walks alone down a litter-strewn alley. In his hand, a coin. He tosses it into the air, once, twice, three times. You know what they say about that number. He sees a homeless man asleep on the ground, his head resting against a bin. Michael throws the coin into the air. As it lands, it hits the rim of the man's cup, which begins to glow like hot iron. The man jolts awake to find himself dressed in a dazzling white suit. His face is stricken, rheumatic eyes shutting once again. He cannot bear the brilliance, the too-white light of transformation.

I feel an affinity with this man. He reads like an avatar for the rabid pop music fan, slumped in the stupor of everyday routine. Along comes a mysterious, glimmering figure who throws everything into light with a single flick of their hand. I often felt blinded by Michael's dazzle, would be left blinking into the relative grey of my actual life, the dreadful normality of everything in it. His music videos offered three-minute blasts of pleasure, images cut and spliced to their most pleasing and saturated, removing the labour of sifting through an uneven world for the beautiful or titillating, and handing me everything at its richest and brightest, buffed to a perfect shine.

When it came to fashion, Michael was a magpie, his clothes fringed and clinking with buckles, sequins and tiny little diamantes. Dude liked to twinkle, as I do. My wardrobe sags with dresses heavy with sequins, gold hoops, brocade, buckles buffed and glowing. Maybe he is why I like such things, feel less than myself when my outfit doesn't wink at everyone I pass. Michael favoured jackets that glowed in the dark, and even his plain white shirts glowed UV clean. In the nineties, he began to favour lamé bodysuits that looked like they were made of padded sheets of foil. It amused me to think that he crinkled as he walked like a Quality Street wrapper.

In these outfits Michael shone, but other times he would become the opposite of light. He would fall down a sudden vacuum, disappearing from sight, leaving the after-print of light in his wake. Moments from music videos play on shutter speed, Michael spinning until he collapses into a pile of fine gold dust. Another time, he morphs into a black panther and disappears behind a lamppost. On stage, his dancers drape him in a bright cloak and he disappears, only to reappear seconds later on a crane above the audience, in a completely new outfit. It was such fun watching him shape-shift, not knowing how or what he would become next.

There was always a surprise hidden in Uncle's hands. He would beckon me over and put his upturned fist in front of my face. His fingers would splay out like a starfish and reveal some small trinket: a beaded bracelet, a bright badge, a lollipop shaped like a flute. Sometimes he'd trick me. I'd prise open his fingers and find his hand empty. *Better luck next time*, he'd say, pinching my nose between his thumb and forefinger.

Once, he took all three of us to the beach in Eastbourne. It was the first time I'd seen the sea. I expected the glittering blue of tropical islands, biscuit-coloured sand I could grip with my toes. But when we got there, the sea was the colour of under-brewed tea, swilling and sighing like it, too, was disappointed in itself. The tide lapped at the ugly pebble beach, hard, round stones pressing into my bare feet. The wind whipped my braids into my face, dashed all the words we said away from us.

Auntie was quiet that day, in one of her inscrutable moods. Something spiky sat between her and Uncle. I went into performance mode, jumping and kicking, singing strange, made-up songs about sentient sea shells. My Shirley Temple act only irritated her further. Though Auntie's sadness wasn't mine, it cast its thick net over us, the whole day, the effort of feigning happiness.

We left Auntie in a café while Uncle took me round the arcade games on the pier. Kids ran around the room, long tails of pink game tokens trailing behind them. I was drawn to the penny slots, the contrast between the dull and shiny coins going in and out like the tide at the beach. I couldn't see the mechanism that made them move back and forth. To my eyes the coins were alive, beckoning.

We tried our luck with the pennies we had, feeding them in. The coins moved forward a millimetre or two, teasing a cascade. Uncle held his last two-pence piece in his hand and closed his fingers over it. *This is the one*, he said. *You need to blow on it, for good luck*. I took a quick gulp of air, blew it out over his knuckles. We both fogged the glass as the coin went in and pushed a row of coins over the edge. It's the sound I imagine plays in the dreams and nightmares of chronic gamblers. It wraps around the ears, the plink-plink-plink of metal kissing metal.

We scooped the coins out with our hands. I couldn't help it: I let out a feral yelp. It can't have been more than a few pounds' worth, but I felt giddy, like we'd won the lottery or robbed a bank. Uncle's face was one big beam. *See that, that's magic. You're magic*, he said. But he was the one who had transformed that coin into a winning one, made a heavy day suddenly joyous.

I thought of this memory after watching James Safechuck describe how Michael would take him shopping for expensive jewellery. There is CCTV footage of the two of them entering a jewellery store with Michael in disguise. Safechuck describes the delight of keeping the rings Michael bought him in a special box. One by one, he holds each ring up to the camera. Under the unforgiving studio lights, the rings seem cheap and tawdry, though they're probably worth thousands of dollars apiece. A once precious memory can turn like oxidised metal. Nothing changes, except the perspective. A slight shift in angle, a sickening of light. In a remarkably steady voice, Safechuck recalls how he once loved these rings, would take them out and admire them, count down the days until he'd get to see Michael again. On screen, he puts them back in their box and shuts the lid, signalling closure. But still he seems racked with disbelief, like an audience member marvelling at a trick they cannot fathom. *How?*

How did he do that?

Star Power

Over and over, I watched the Motown twenty-fifth anniversary performance, relishing the pause before the glide, the delayed screams of the audience as Michael moved as if pushed back by an invisible hand. He was even dressed like a magician, with his white glove and black jacket, the sequinned wink of his socks. He pulled straight from the playbook of the Messiah. Just as Jesus walked on water, Michael walked on the moon. Both sought to prove themselves beyond the mortal shackles of logic, but Michael was not a story in a leather-bound book or a heavy sermon relayed from a distant pulpit. He was a living and breathing miracle in my midst.

The earliest recorded instance of the moonwalk was in 1932, when entertainer Cab Calloway called it 'the buzz'. But Michael is credited with taking this move and not only perfecting it but renaming it from 'the backslide' to 'the moonwalk'. This stroke of branding genius takes our mind away from the mechanics of the move and to its associative power to transcend itself.

By the time Michael did the moonwalk on national TV in 1983, it had been only fourteen years since Neil Armstrong had taken his fateful steps on the Moon, a moment that is still shrouded with conspiracy and speculation. In renaming the dance, Michael placed himself in a lineage of crusaders and pioneers, men who placed themselves at the centre of era-defining moments.

Witnessing a well-executed moonwalk is realising the defiance of the human body, how it flirts with and pushes against gravity, temporal space, physiological limits. Many of Michael's signature moves have this quality. I remember swooning at how he dragged his feet across the floor like a soft paintbrush against canvas. He would spin himself into a blur, then, suddenly, his slight body would freeze faithful as a photo as he stood on his toes. Always, I returned to the moonwalk, how he managed to better it in 1995 at the MTV Awards, the transition from spin to slide even more seamless, his body seemingly exerting no effort.

The moonwalk is, first and foremost, a failure of information. Like many visually satisfying dance moves, it relies on the strategic transfer of a dancer's weight. The moonwalk is not magic. It is a glorious scam, art made in the gap between what our eyes see and what our brains tell us.

In a bid to understand the science further, I've been forced to engage with physics. I squint at my screen in latent panic at phrases like 'the co-efficient of kinetic friction' and 'r 2 – r 1 is less than r 1 and N 1 will be larger than N 2'. What I largely glean is this: the moonwalk's magic is dependent on a subtle manipulation of how we perceive stationary and moving forces. Have you ever been sat on a still train when another train on the opposite track starts moving? You may recall that unnerving feeling that it is *your* train that's moving. The mind and body briefly mimics the sensation of forward motion before the brain recalibrates and a sense of stillness returns. This happens because the mind collates what it sees and feels to correspond with what is most likely. The moonwalk, then, works like many magic tricks by exploiting the limitations of the human brain.

The world is far too complex and stimulating for us to take in every detail. Most of what we consider 'seeing' is actually just projected expectation. Every second, our brains are filling in the big picture based on our best guesses of what should logically be in front of us. This is the central tenet of the law of good continuation, a concept coined by German Gestalt psychologists at the turn of the century. Take, for example, watching a ventriloquist act. You hear a voice the same time as the mouth of the puppet is moving. If the ventriloquist is especially skilled, the puppet's mouth will stretch and pucker in time with the words while the puppet master's mouth appears to be closed. This input collates in the brain to create the most logically and narratively pleasing idea: that the puppet is speaking. Though we know how a ventriloquist act works, we are committed to the coherence of the illusion in front of us. The illusion is collaborative between puppet and master, master and audience. We know we're being tricked, but we don't quite know how. This tension keeps us looking and looking again, perplexed yet delighted by our own deception. But if we detect even a micro movement of the master's lip, we feel betrayed. All parties have committed to the greater good of the entertaining lie.

Michael's famous lean from the 'Smooth Criminal' video is another vertiginous wonder. His body falls forwards, a slow-motion pratfall that somehow evades disaster. Instead of hitting the ground, he hovers mere inches from the floor. In watching it, a world order is shattered. Gravity is a trickster, building alliances with people wily enough to call its bluff. The viewer must make up their mind as to how this impossible thing is happening. Clive told me it was strings suspended from the ceiling that held him in place. I wasn't convinced by this, holding instead to the more magical idea that Newtonian physics simply didn't apply to Michael's body.

Neither of us were right, but the truth is closer to Clive's hypothesis than mine. To perform the lean live, Michael wears a special pair of patented shoes that slot into a protruding piece of metal on the stage. Just before the move is executed, the slot emerges from the floor. To shift the audience's gaze away from this moment of preparation, the lights go down on

Michael's side of the stage and come up on a performer who artfully distracts us with sparklers in either hand, their body undulating like a snake charmer. The light from the sparklers makes bright S shapes in the air. Dumb as moths, we follow the sparklers' trajectory before the lights switch focus again. Michael and his dancers are ready by this point, their shoes firmly slotted into place. They lean forward until their faces are inches from the floor and hold the pose.

As an adult, I share this revelation with Clive who refuses to believe the truth of how 'the lean' works, insisting on his string theory. We enjoy the pantomime of bickering for a few minutes, though I suspect neither of us is totally wedded to our stance. Holding fast to our pet theories is easier than accepting that we'll never know for sure.

On YouTube, I find a compilation that traces the moonwalk's evolution. Grainy footage of black men in zoot suits, fleet of foot and jolly of face. They perform early versions of not just the moonwalk, but so many of the moves that have become indelibly associated with Michael. The leg kicks, the turns, the soft shoe shuffles that tap dancers of the vaudeville days perfected. I watch the clips from MGM films that Michael borrowed from, often ripping entire scenes and recreating them for his music videos. His foot sweep is Gene Kelly's, his jazz shuffle Fosse's. When he dramatically falls to his knees on stage, it's with the same drama of his idol James Brown. He took entire concepts for his videos from old Rat Pack films and schlocky horror movies. Yes, Michael was a singular artist, but he was also a beady-eyed student and shrewd curator.

Michael's star rose such that his influences were swallowed

and muted. When something wows us, we assume we are seeing something new and original. This is bolstered by the gaps in our knowledge, the overwhelming dominance of a handful of stars and their opacity in acknowledging their references. We don't want to know that the thing we love is borrowed or derivative. A magic trick is never as dazzling as the first time you saw it. I've found myself disappointed after learning that so many of Michael's ideas were built on homages and references. Of course, this is simply how culture works. All artists wear their references, consciously or not, and it's this palimpsest of ideas that makes being an artist inherently collaborative and conversational.

But this idea disrupts the romantic notion of the lone genius, whose unique ideas visit him, unbidden, as a gift from the Muses. Michael spoke about music-making in vague, mystical terms, stating that his talent was god-given and thus indefinable. His approach to writing was to 'get out of the way' and wait for the music to announce itself. Entire songs, he said, would come to him in dreams. It's true that much of the creative process is shadowy, eludes formula and analysis. We each have different words for what lives in this space and some see fit to call it god. An artist's narrative about process is a revealing piece of art in and of itself. It's less exciting to consider that art might simply be the result of obsessive study and technical prowess.

Rarely did Michael allow his audience to see the nuts and bolts that made his stage persona. But later in his career, the slickness he insisted on began to loosen. In a disarming moment in the *HIStory* tour, Michael strolls on stage holding an old-fashioned canvas suitcase. It is not the assured stride of a performer before he hits his spot. He looks to his left then his right, as if he wandered on stage by mistake. He is performing aimlessness, the listless ways of a nondescript man. He puts the suitcase down and sits on it, as if waiting for a bus. The audience's cheers falter then start to subside. Their impatience simmers like a veiled threat. The King of Pop has been replaced by an interloper, some awkward teenager who's made the rash decision to run away from home.

Eventually, he stands up and places the suitcase on a small table. With an uncharacteristic lack of ceremony, he opens it and takes out three items. First, his sequinned black jacket. At this, the crowd wakes back up. He is transforming before their eyes. He slings the jacket on, shrugging his shoulders up and down as if trying it on for the first time. Second comes a white sequinned glove, which inspires a different pitch of screams from the crowd. On Michael's face, a brief smile. It's a playful moment of self-referential theatre, the equivalent of a knowing wink to camera. In previous tours, he would arrive for 'Billie Jean' fully costumed and ready to hit his iconic beginning pose with his hat over his face, his body bent and taut as a bracket.

Here, we get to watch how the magic happens. We witness how each element, mundane and impotent in isolation, creates the icon. The jacket animates his shoulders, which undulate beneath their sheath of sequins. Inside the glove, his fingers flex and wiggle. The black hat is the final part. Michael looks down at it in his hand, milking the moment. The crowd is now in a frenzy, a willing co-creator in this blissful tension. By now, they know what's coming next, but are no less thrilled for it. The symbolic resonance of each item is not just in the reveal, but in every performance that's come before this moment. The suitcase acts like a time capsule in which layer after layer of overlapping performances of 'Billie Jean' sit. Here is every time he has performed this song and the first time each person in the 120,000-strong audience saw it for the first time. Michael was never an artist who bargained with the tools of relatability. There is never any relaxed patter between songs or stripped-back acoustic numbers sung at a humble stool. Michael was slick, celestial and staunchly perfectionist, accounting for every ad lib, scene change and dance move. He showed everything and revealed nothing. Even this suitcase moment was its own artifice, but it still stands out as a rare and fascinating instance where Michael allows the magic to happen *with* rather than *to* us. When the drums of the intro finally descend, the look behind the curtain hasn't shattered the illusion. It has illuminated something honest about the process of self-creation. In honouring the artifice of his craft, Michael offers a rare moment of honesty that heightens rather than undermines his magical aura.

Art, and music in particular, feels like the last bastion of magic permitted to the weary adult. Even the most unsentimental among us gladly succumbs to the joys of a song that speaks to some deep, unspoken part of us. It makes sense, then, that our reverence for the music we love extends to the musicians who make it. Without them, these moments would not exist, or at least not in the specific iteration that could only come from them. We both identify with and aspire to the clarity of feeling in a lyric or chord progression.

But why this intense identification with our favourite singers? Certainly, the commercial machine creates and encourages this porosity between art and artist. They only stand to make more money from our parasocial desire to 'connect' with the artists we admire. Of course, it's possible to connect deeply with a piece of music while knowing nothing about the artist. But for me, it's second nature to look up the person who made something that's moved me. The desire to match the art to its maker is immediate, especially now with the frightening ease of an internet search.

Constantly, we are searching for our emotional kin. It's part of why we make and seek out art in the first place. When I hear a song for the first time and its lyrics resonate, I want to know if the artist and I share any characteristics or life experiences. Sometimes the bridge between us is thin, yet still meaningful in its own way. We might be a similar age or have a similar face. But it's more interesting when the artist is nothing like me on the surface, yet something in the way they phrase their sorrows or pluck at their guitar feels like some part of me has shaken itself loose and found itself in someone else's throat.

The musicians we love are some of the only magical figures we're allowed as we grow up. One by one, the others are robbed from us. The tooth fairy is killed by the discovery of baby teeth in a jar, the slip of a false beard reveals Santa as fake. We learn an unsettling truth that authority figures will lie to us, repeatedly, in service to a magical story.

I fall in love with artists when their work moves me because they do something we often fail to do in our daily interactions with each other: tell the truth. The artist parts the curtains that separate us from our true feelings. They reach through an inexpressible tangle of thought or feeling and create vibrations of sound, an effusive stroke of paint, an arabesque, a poetic image that makes us say *yes, that is it. That is it, exactly.*

Transformative art is us at our most focused and fully feeling. In the sheer act of creating, even the most depressed or depraved artist writes a love letter to being alive. I can't shake the conviction that art is often better, more loving and brave than the humans who make it. At its best, it offers the most beautiful and succinct insight into how a person sees the world, without the burden of interacting with them.

When I voiced this thought to a friend she laughed an awkward, hollow laugh, and in it I heard myself through her nervous reaction. I felt suddenly exposed and tried to palm the statement off as tongue in cheek. But I believe it. Where people flounder, art flourishes. Before you label me a sociopath, let me say: I do love people. They really can be wonderful, in spite of themselves. But they are also intolerably messy, a tangle of self-effacing lies and contradictions. I know this because I see it and hate it in myself. But always there's the sweet relief of art. A book can be picked up and set down, a song can be paused. But I cannot pause, rewind, turn up or overwrite a person, no matter how mad, bad or cruel.

One of the best and most dangerous things about humans is our bent for storytelling. Any given object means as much or as little as we decide it does. I don't think it's an accident that magical thinking is experiencing a renaissance. We've been abandoned by the bearded gods of the Bible, the suited bosses of the banks. In this existential gulf, magic is asked to do more than just distract us. We want transcendence, some sign that there is more than the random onslaught of moments that make a life.

Ever since my obsession with Michael waned, and the reality of his actions came to bear, it's been hard to trust myself with anything akin to worship. I'm scared to have feelings of awe or excitement about any person or thing. I can't even look up at the moon without feeling betrayed. It hangs there bright, white, fickle as a promise.

Despite my false start in the now defunct Honey Girlz, I eventually did find my niche as a professional performer. It was in the glamorous and famously well-paid world of performance poetry that I flourished. On most days, I am interacting with performers of all walks. Poets, singers, rappers, musicians, actors, comedians, dancers, strippers. If it's done on stage, I probably know someone who does it professionally. I'd be hard pressed to pick out a common trait amongst us, and contrary to popular belief many accomplished performers are introverted types. But I do wonder at this shared compulsion of ours. What compels a person to demand a crowd's attention?

A good performance unfolds like mass hypnosis. I use a common technique, a bait and switch of reliability and exceptionalism. *I'm just like you* is the opening gambit and constant touch point. *But I am also different, special, shinier than the rest of you.* This thought, unconscious or not, is made explicit by the set-up. One person, on a raised platform, amplified and spotlit, everyone else a pliant witness.

Many times, I've watched someone with a magnetic stage presence and felt an immediate and private rapport with them, undisrupted by all the other people in the crowd I'm sharing them with. *If we met*, I tell myself, *we would be friends*. But the traits that make an electric performer don't necessarily translate in offstage interactions. A person who's charming onstage can make for a self-obsessed friend or manipulative lover off stage.

I assume it's a hard thing to imagine, or sympathise with, if this is the opposite of your temperament. But all I'll say is it's a soft power, this ability to get an audience on side. It's a highly addictive feeling that distorts and inflates your sense of self. Yes, there are narcissistic traces in every performer. It is impossible to do this job well without a healthy dose of self-regard, a persistent belief in your potential brilliance. But any hope of functioning relationships rests on remembering the ultimate farce of the endeavour. Daily, I remind myself how weird it is to demand the sustained gaze and attention of strangers, not only often but for a living! *She's a bit of a show-off, isn't she?* You must take yourself extremely seriously one moment, then laugh the next.

Even in the lopsided context of a stage show, a meaningful connection between performer and audience is possible. Some of the moments I hold closest to my heart happened with me on a stage or in a crowd. But what passes between that membrane is not love. The problem is that it really can feel like it, or at least the giddy, immature kind we court as teenagers. It's the same heady rush of adrenaline and limerence, where nagging thoughts of the past or the future disappear. For those who spend months at a time touring, clocking hours and hours on stage, it's life off stage that begins to feel surreal and disconcerting. The stage becomes your life blood, the only time you feel like yourself.

In Mary Shelley's *Frankenstein*, the doctor's original vision was not to make a monster. He intended to make a beautiful man from the best body parts he could scavenge from his graveyard digs. This man would be exemplary: strong, intelligent and classically handsome. But the end result of Frankenstein's experiment was a grotesque creature who was all the more hideous for his proximity to beauty. Michael's face was also an eerie assemblage of features pulled from a cartoon of the all-American pop star. His chin cleft deepened and deepened until it sank into itself. His cheekbones poked out like a resourceful squirrel's in winter. And that hair. The curled black wigs that became shinier and more coiffed as the Jheri curl of the eighties became a long smooth bob in the nineties. The more perfectly placed on his head they were, the more improbable they looked.

The beginning of the 'Thriller' video unfolds like a harbinger. 'I'm not like other guys,' Michael whispers before his face begins to warp, growing molten wrinkles and thick whiskers. His lover screams an endless scream as his diminutive features coarsen. His dark eyes suddenly glow streetlight yellow, with slitted pupils like a snake's. The director John Landis explained that the aim was for this mutation to be dramatic and scary, but not ugly. The volcanic contours of the mask still retained the structure of a classically handsome face, with a strong jaw and proud cheekbones. The result is a face that's disturbing to look at yet impossible to pull your eyes from.

Michael recalled one of his first sightings of transformation on a stage, when he was still a child: 'I had seen quite a few strippers, but that night this one girl with gorgeous eyelashes and long hair came out and did her routine. She put on a great performance. All of a sudden, at the end, she took off her wig, pulled a pair of big oranges out of her bra, and revealed that she was a hard-faced guy under all that make-up. That blew me away.'

I come unstuck at the slippery use of pronouns, how even at that tender age Michael did not feel deceived or tricked by this performance, but transported and inspired. He would go on to have a lifelong fascination with disguise, one that dripped into the visuals for his videos and his tactics for evading the public. Early in his career, he would don a disguise to knock on doors as a Jehovah's Witness. As his fame grew, he used wigs, glasses and sometimes a prosthetic nose to get around without being noticed. He got a kick out of these moments where he eluded the public gaze. It was impossible for him to walk down a street without getting recognised and possibly harassed. He'd been living with this hypervisibility from the age of nine. By the time he was a teenager, he was mortified by his changing appearance, especially the angry red acne that he desperately covered with make-up. It's easy to see how this lifelong affair with disguises was a source of mischief, as well as a much needed escape from the pressures of fame.

As a child, I felt certain that if I were to slice Michael open, like magicians do their glamorous assistants, I wouldn't find bones, blood or an intestinal tract, and certainly nothing as homely as a pancreas. There'd be organs and apparitions for which we don't have names. Michael and I were not made of the same stuff, and that was the crucial axis on which my love stood.

In the face of dazzling talent, we implicitly trust this person who has brought some ineffable part of our humanity to the surface. Their talent feels like virtue. Learning about any less than honourable behaviour on their part forces us to confront the gulf between the person and the persona. Before the onset of celebrity culture as we now understand it, largely precipitated by photography and interviews, the debate of separating the art from the artist was less pertinent to the average person. A star's image was not so closely welded to their art in the way it is now. It was entirely possible to listen to a piece of music and have little or no idea of who the artist was or what they looked like. The continuum between known person and good person began as a growing media machine took note of how many papers and magazines could be sold if investment in the lives of celebrities was encouraged.

Fast-forward to our current, oxymoronic time, where the 'personal brand' of the influencer has created yet another echelon of celebrity, and with it more ways for us to follow and project on to the lives of perfect strangers. Though our critique of this culture is growing sharper, we seem no closer to a reckoning of how this valorising of celebrity has warped our moral compass. John Keats once said that 'beauty is truth and truth beauty', an adage that speaks to our frightening tendency to assume someone is good purely because we love their music, their appearance, the facade of how they present themselves to the public. Celebrities in turn make sure stories of their good deeds reach the press, ostensibly to 'raise awareness' but also to furnish their image as role models.

What spell did Michael weave on me? Like any good magic trick, I cannot trace the seams of its workings. I was willing, suggestible, like children are allowed to be. Michael took great pains to paint himself as wholly good, harmlessly eccentric. His wispy speaking voice and shyness in interviews hardly signalled malice. He had a pet chimp called Bubbles, for god's sake. There was also the coterie of A-list friends whose accumulative glow created an almost blinding halo of goodwill above him.

Michael as a potential human did not interest me. Like an audience member committed to the illusion, I did not care to see the things that didn't add up. Through him, I could conjure and sustain mystery and awe. I liked that no conclusive answers could ever be drawn about who, or what, Michael was.

Michael's songs don't sound the same any more, but I still play them. I am trying to perform the hardest trick of all: time travel. I want to go back to before I knew what I know now, and stay there, suspended in the moment before the reveal. Give me back the lie, the gentle sedative of denial. Maybe it's the truth that is cruel, the truth that's the trick. There is no such thing as magic, after all. There is only the information we do not have, the things we choose not to see.

Suspend Your Disbelief

Once again, I soothe my friend Maya over the phone. She is beside herself wondering why the man she's seeing has turned out to be another non-starter. She explains that he is everything she wants: charming, educated, can pull off a pair of corduroys. She was smitten, and in a tale old as Tinder, the more enamoured she felt, the more distant he became. I steel myself to give advice I know will be completely disregarded. Just from her tone of voice I know she has already decided who she needs this man to be for her own sanity. Everything he did from that point, no matter how at odds with that fantasy, would be bent and twisted until it fit.

This is why I take a little vial of scepticism with me everywhere. It's crucial, especially when you find yourself immediately and fatally attracted to the person waiting for you at the bar. Someone's so much easier to believe, aren't they, when you're wondering how much tongue they're partial to using when they kiss? By that point, you're a goner. You laugh before they've even landed the punchline of their joke. All of their anecdotes strike you as uniquely novel and engrossing. Even the sweat patch under their left arm is in the shape of a heart. You know kismet when you see it!

Then, of course, your senses take their leave after the second pint and now you're halfway into the fourth, laughing at a meme you don't understand. The man could do something unforgivable, like take out a deck of cards and insist on doing a two-bit trick and you would find it ironically charming. Vigilance is key. You don't want the personality profile of someone who'd be selected to volunteer for a televised mind reading. These people, sorry to say it, are mugs. They don't just suspend their disbelief. They toss it over their shoulder.

Magic, like romantic love, buoys us with its shrouds of mystery, the push-pull of foreboding and excitement. Knowingly and unknowingly, we invest in love as a happening rather than a physiological occurrence. What we register as 'instant connection' and 'love at first sight' usually exposes something more banal about our behavioural patterns and psychic wounds.

The madness of an all-encompassing crush starts to make more sense when seen through the law of good continuation. A crush is someone who we fancy and usually don't know very well. They become the perfect site for our projections. Ultimately, we see what we want to see in that person. The heart is desperate to match its desire for love with the person we think should give it to us. This is how Maya has ended up in her hopeless predicament. We work with what we have to create the story we wish to live in, whether the people we choose as characters are willing participants or not.

The feeling of familiarity that stokes the rush of strong, initial attraction is of course impossible to nail with language, hence why it feels so overwhelming. But we are much more predictable and herd-like in our choices than we might think. In the object of our affections is usually the ghost of a father whose approval we never quite won, an overprotective mother or an ex whose hair colour reprises itself in every person we've dated since.

We turn to the science of love to try and make sense of all of this, to feel comforted by the partial answers therein. But the thing that mythologises and sustains love is the language we use, and this language is steeped in mythology and the supernatural. We talk of fate and destiny, grand words that pull us back to when we wished on stars and tucked milk teeth under our pillows for the tooth fairy.

Pop stars have long toyed with this performance of intimacy with their audience, breaking the fourth wall between the stage and the crowd. Closing this gap disrupts the imagined view between gods and mortals. When the performer approaches the front row and runs their palm down a line of waiting hands, they are Jesus pointing to his stigmata. *Look*, this gesture says, *I am the fabled man made flesh*.

Michael found me at an age and time where I was prime for such a bewitching. It sometimes felt romantic, other times softer and more paternal. Wade Robson described Michael as a quasi-caretaker in his home – a figure forever present on the TV, keeping watch from the posters on his bedroom wall.

Michael felt like an extra parental figure to me, too. I loved and trusted him without question, like any child does their parents.

We like the idea that we are creatures of mystical whim rather than animals led by synaptic responses. Perhaps we deliberately minimise our ability to analyse our situation and make reasonable decisions. It is more freeing to rescind our power. We tell ourselves we 'cannot help' who we love or how we love, a seductive idea and a dangerous cop-out.

When creating his lavish stage shows, Michael often sought the expertise of professional magicians and illusionists, some of whom became personal friends. One of those was Uri Geller, one of the most well-known and controversial magicians of the late twentieth century. The two were friends right up until Michael's death, with Michael performing best man duties at Geller's wedding. Geller came to prominence in the seventies with his purported powers of psychokinesis and telepathy, which he used to bend spoons and stop clocks. He claimed some pretty bonkers stuff, including that he'd been sent to Earth by aliens living 53,000 light years away. The American public bit, and he did the rounds on a scatter of talk shows. He was catnip for these audiences, with his good looks and easy charm. He even had the CIA study his 'telepathic' abilities, which they concluded were 'convincing and unambiguous'.

But his ascendance hit a glitch in 1973 when a planned appearance on *The Tonight Show Starring Johnny Carson* went awry. Suspicion around the legitimacy of Geller's tricks was growing louder, so the show's production team had his aluminium props painted with a thin layer of cement underneath so they couldn't move. As was suspected, the subtle movement of the pieces was a crucial part of how Geller could pull off the illusion of the spoons bending. After trying and failing to do the trick live on TV, Geller was briefly a laughing stock. Believing himself irreversibly shamed, he made plans to return to his home country of Israel to regroup and lick his wounds.

But just before he got on the flight, he got a phone call: it was an invite to go on another talk show. In later interviews, he would say that this was a pivotal moment in his career. It dawned on him that being a successful magician is not about the unwavering success of your tricks. It turned out that the doubt and the swirling of rumour didn't undermine his act. It only added to the intrigue. Was he really magic or just an opportunist? Whether people derided or lauded him, he had become the test for people's parameters of belief. As Corrieri puts it, magic is 'fundamentally a form of meta-theatre: intensely and inherently self-reflexive, its raison d'être consists in spectators questioning the act itself'.

Michael, too, was wily and strategic in his use of people's scepticism. Early in his career, he played into many of the outlandish rumours about him, even encouraging his PR team to fan the flames. Compared to the much darker headlines that Michael would be plagued with in the post-*HIStory* era, the ones printed in the eighties were fun and somewhat camp. While people wondered if Michael had bought the bones of the Elephant Man or slept in an oxygen chamber, the fact was that his name was on people's lips. Uri Geller also rode his infamy into a long career of appearances and shows spanning decades.

Meanwhile, a man named James Randi watched on with

growing frustration. Randi was a first-class rider on the Geller hate train. He thought Geller was a hack and a chancer, a shameless manipulator of his gullible audience. Randi was also a professional magician, but unlike Geller he was a staunch rationalist. Fed up with the wild claims from self-defined psychics, mediums and mystics, Randi made it his life's work to disprove any claims of the supernatural, even offering a million-dollar prize to anyone who could provide evidence of the supernatural under mutually agreed test conditions. He would eventually write and publish a whole book (*The Truth About Uri Geller*) exposing the fraudulence of Geller's claims to magical powers.

Randi and Geller represent two very different approaches to courting the public. Randi appeals to our rational minds, imploring us to be critical and cautious. There is nothing jovial or flirty in his demeanour. Geller, by contrast, reels us in with his unassuming boyishness and lilting Israeli accent (exotic enough to thrill, but not so foreign as to strike fear in the hearts of Middle America). He has a telegenic presence and loves the rapt attention of an audience. Magic is always helped along by aesthetics. Even Randi begrudgingly conceded that Geller's attractiveness aided him in his career. Presumably through gritted teeth, he described Geller as 'beautiful, affectionate, genuine, forward-going, handsome – everything!'

Randi, bless him, was not a heart throb. His was a stern, headmasterly presence that instinctively makes you sit up straighter. Though his glasses and bright white beard give him the gravitas of an aged wizard, he speaks with the nasal wheedle of a nerdy professor. He was power-shy and unmoved by the idea of fame. He believed performing magic without explaining the methods at hand was inherently exploitative.

Though he tirelessly campaigned against the spurious claims of other magicians, his appeals to science were no match for the burning desire of many to believe in magic. There will always be the audience members who, like me, take pleasure in looking for the mechanisms of a trick, even if it eludes them. But then there are those who lead with belief, what illusionist Derren Brown calls the 'highly suggestible'. This group willingly colludes with a trick, ignoring any signs that point to subterfuge.

To his horror, Randi found that even when he explained that he wasn't magic, audience members would write to him after his shows and insist that he was. His rationality could not cut through the zealous belief of these people. They had already made up their minds about who he was and what they saw in him. No matter how overwhelming the evidence we are given, if we sense the emotional cost of accepting the truth will be too high, we will live with the lie instead. Deceit is often consensual. We jealously reserve the right to our own delusions.

At what age does it become uncool to hire a magician for your birthday party? I surveyed my friends on this, who surprised me with the strength of their varying opinions. The debate raged for some minutes, before they settled on the age of nine, the tipping point when a child confronts the onset of puberty. It makes sense. This is right about when self-consciousness ramps up. New and overwhelming fears abound about every choice, and conformity is the best armour. Magicians become suddenly and unequivocally lame. But a five-year-old cares not a jot for this, delighted by the smiley man who makes animals out of balloons, pulls a flourish of coloured scarves from a hat. But by nine years old, the magician's act starts to feel cloying. As we enter early adulthood, the magician slides further down in our estimations, downgraded to the category of Unironic Sleaze. And so it was with Michael. At first, my love for him was understood and encouraged. Then it became embarrassing, something I ought to have outgrown. Now, it's unambiguously shameful, covered in a thick film of slime. Just the mention of his name inspires shudders, a pitying wince.

Though we all agreed there was a long exodus in which a magician's presence was unwelcome, we also decided that after many decades in the cold a magician might find a grateful audience again, this time with the seventy-plus crowd. By then, we don't care for what's cool or socially sanctioned: we are happy to allow ourselves the nostalgic pleasure of cheap delights. Maybe I'll return to Michael this way, in my old age. I'll circle right back to my early, childlike wonder. I'll let my mouth fall open in a round O of awe, my memory wiped of all its snags and tensions.

Loving Michael, like the best feats of magic, was easy. It was scarcely a decision. I showed up wide-eyed, willing. Highly suggestible. It was exactly what I was told love would be: focused, involuntary, all-consuming. It grew with me, from a childlike wonder to a voracious want. My obsession had its own puberty, growing suddenly physical and unruly. It wasn't sexual per se, but it had its own erotic charge, a restlessness that made me newly aware of my body and its troubling transformation. It was no longer enough to reach my idol through the mediation of a screen or headphones. I wanted to see the whites of his eyes, the tremble of his hands, the sweat on his brow and the heave of his chest that confirmed yes, this is real, he exists. He is not some figment of your feral imagination, no trick of the light.

DESIRE

Never Washing My Hand Again

I am twenty-four, with my own money that I earn in a tiny café on the posh side of the city. I have a small but not insignificant pot of funds to spend on things that delight me: dangly earrings, multipacks of McCoy's crisps and gig tickets. Maya and I decide to go to a concert of yet another pop star I have grown untenably attached to. This one is black, too, like Michael, but she has remained so. She is also larger than life, impossibly theatrical, and seems to feel safest when embodying an elaborate persona. She wears tailored tuxedo suits and her feet move busy as brooms across the floor. Best of all is the fat exclamation point of her hair. I battle with gravity and several cans of hairspray to get mine the same shape and height. The potential of my own beauty feels less preposterous, simply because she exists. This gig was going to be a good time. It was going to be a pilgrimage.

We get ready in Maya's room, which is larger than mine with a better, full-length mirror. We met and became friends at university. It was a time of flux, full of trials in taste and personality. We bore witness to each other's many artless attempts at becoming. We have worn each other's tops and borrowed each other's politics. I introduced her to Janelle Monáe, and now she loves her just as much as me. As we have on many other nights like this, we get ready to go out together. Getting ready is my favourite cliché about girlhood. I'm in love with its intricate choreography: the clothes piling up like unfinished thoughts on the carpet, the sickening swirl of anticipation just as sweet as it was at the Year Six school disco, that first freshers' club night. Things have changed slightly. What was once the thick meld of cheap, competing body sprays is a swirl of slightly more expensive perfumes. I use the same cheap straighteners of my pre-teen years, but I am not forcing my hair down into thin, straight wisps, praying they touch my shoulders. Now, I swoop my hair heavenward, praying it won't deflate with the heat and sweat in the venue. Janelle sings from Maya's tiny Bluetooth speaker and we swap germs from the same clumped mascara wand, sing along to the songs we're about to see live. Long live the romance of sharing make-up and swigs from the same bottle of vinegary wine. It's a nice change, sharing an obsession with someone. Janelle added to the growing lore of our friendship, gave us a joint language and mission.

When we get inside, the vibe is not what we expected. It feels collegiate, sensible. There are a lot of white people. Purse-lipped. Parent-aged. Maya and I look at each other, bemused. I feel suddenly stupid in my quiff, which Maya has to periodically shift with her fingers to keep it from drooping.

Everyone politely waits their turn at the bar. People say *excuse me* as they wriggle through the crowds. We watch the serviceable support act and nurse plastic pints while we wait for the main act. When Janelle finally arrives, the room holds its breath. For the two hours leading up to this, we've restlessly shifted from foot to foot, swayed and dawdled, bent our necks to check the time on our phones. Now we surge towards the stage like a wave, pressing our collective weight against the barrier. Maya and I squeal like schoolgirls, reach for each other's hands and squeeze. We bump against backpacks and elbows, every gap between our bodies closed. In my nose, the not unpleasant funk of spilt cider, dry ice, cologne. I am moved and reassured by gentle wafts of BO. We are in it, committed, up against each other for the night. For the next two hours, we will move like a single organism.

Janelle is here. We forget our brains, remember our bodies.

We dance.

We sing.

We scream.

Maya's face is glazed, her brown eyes mascara-flecked and glistening. She is gorgeous, as am I and the balding dad in his band T-shirt next to us and his rosy-cheeked wife. Janelle is the preacher and we are her loyal congregation. We cheer when told, a thick, piercing wall of sound. We jump up and bend low as one, sway our arms left to right like long grass in a stiff breeze.

Janelle works us to a crescendo, then, for the final song, launches herself into the crowd. I assess my position with the precision of a sniper. Each of her limbs are splayed out starfish wide as we gently sink to absorb her weight. Her body rises and falls on our choppy tide. I note that I'm in a good place. Maya is behind me, out of my sight and focus. My position is perfect. I have time and room to manoeuvre according to where the crowd carries her. In front of me, the soles of her feet loom. Her trousers are dark and cleave close to her legs. It's a good amount of surface area, all to play for. I shuffle slightly to the left, in the direction she's floating in. But the people closest to me have had the same thought, and for a moment I'm crushed by their desperate scrabble. I wriggle and shuffle, get myself back to a prime position. Maybe I can catch her on her way back to the stage. My hand will touch some part of her body and this, I'm convinced, will confirm my unique affinity with Janelle. My pilgrimage will be complete.

But then, disaster. She begins to pivot. Her face betrays a twitch of anxiety. Someone has grabbed her a little too firmly, perhaps. God knows the places hands could traverse in a moment like this. A quick glance is exchanged between her and the security guard by the barriers. She's about to be hauled back on stage. I will lose my moment, my Mecca. I can hear Maya calling my name but I ignore her. Wedging my body between the two bodies in front of me, I am juiced up by a new and unfamiliar force. I have to reach her. I have to. In touching distance, her long feet in their black boots bob like a pair of buoys. This close, I can see the hint of a blemish under her make-up, two small scuffs on her right shoe. Like the leper reaching for Jesus' garment, I extend my fingers, wish them longer, more dexterous. It happens, just, not quite . . . Yes! Contact! A brush against rubber sole. I squeeze, let go, like testing a mango's ripeness. I felt it, the unmistakeable warmth of the foot under the leather. It is the greatest thing I've ever achieved, I'm certain of it. And she felt it, surely, the distinctness of my touch. Others around me reach and lurch, throw their arms forward and fail. Too bad, too bad, they have failed The

Test. I hear my name, right by my ear this time. I think for a moment that it's Janelle calling out for me. But Maya's hands grip my shoulders. She roughly tilts me back, yells into my ear. *If you ever wash that hand again, I'm kicking you out of the house.* I press my hot palm to her cheek. We shriek.

In his excoriating takedown of Beatlemania and the legions of mostly female fans that formed it, the journalist Paul Johnson wrote:

> While the music is performed, the cameras linger savagely over the faces of the audience. What a bottomless chasm of vacuity they reveal! The huge faces, bloated with cheap confectionery and smeared with chain-store makeup, the open, sagging mouths and glazed eyes, the broken stiletto heels: here is a generation enslaved by a commercial machine.

I know and love this scene. Honestly, I feel slightly gleeful at the terror girls like us inspire in this man, try as he might to disguise his fear as worldly disdain. His is a weirdly baroque brand of misogyny, one that imagines girls like me and Maya as zombies sent to crush moral decency under our 'broken stiletto heels'. Instead of enquiring as to the inner lives of these girls and why they behave as they do, he reduces them to brain-dead corpses. How incurious and cruel. How dull!

It is supposed to read as a warning of pending cultural dystopia. In me, it presses different pulse points. I am never more aware of my body than when it's smushed up against uncountable others, the press of a full bladder lending urgency to every move. How the thirst in your throat and ache in your legs disappears as soon as the music starts. I love the hitch in my voice as the lights dim and the silhouette of a long-awaited star appears. And I love lying in bed afterwards, nursing the residual ache in my temples from all that screaming, the ringing in my ears like an echo beckoning me back to the madness.

In 1995, I am four years old, oblivious to Michael's existence. This is probably for the best, as at the time his reputation was at an all-time low. Having settled the first spate of assault allegations out of court, he hastily married Lisa Marie Presley, just twenty days after her divorce from Danny Keough was finalised. PR stunt or not, this played out poorly in the public sphere. They both did the media rounds, their matching red lips stretched into dazed smiles. Lisa Marie came off like a beard, forced to defend their relationship in a series of painfully stilted interviews. Michael blundered his way through probing questions about their sex life, giggling and squirming like a sheltered pre-teen. This attempt to portray himself as innocent, normal and straight was disastrous, doing more to confirm rather than suppress the public's suspicions.

In a desperate attempt to rehabilitate his icon status, the campaign for the *HIStory* album doubled down on Michael as a beleaguered hero sabotaged by his money-hungry enemies. We were to believe he was targeted because he was too powerful, too brilliant. In service to this, a promotional compilation video was made called 'Brace Yourself'. Watching it evokes the same feverish delirium I get after drinking three strong coffees in quick succession. Its backing track is 'O Fortuna/Carmina Burana', the same song that Simon Cowell and his merry men of judges would walk out to on the *X Factor* live shows. It's ridiculously pompous, a level of Wagnerian camp that's impossible to take seriously. And yet. From the first clash of the grand symbol, my heart starts glitching. For its entire three-minute duration, I am seized with a delicious panic, the kind you might feel watching a tightrope walker above a pool of sharks. It's a breathlessly over the top piece of propaganda, each clip selected for maximum drama. One moment he is shyly waving to legions of screaming fans who run after his car, the next he is flanked by a platoon of soldiers and marching towards a slowly filling stadium. Banners displaying the names of different cities flash across the screen: Köln, Paris, Barcelona. World dominance is the implication, but record sales for *HIStory* indicated the American public had fallen far more out of love with Michael than their European counterparts. This display is less of a flex and more a careful hedging of bets.

From the front row of his concerts, the fans writhe and thrash in orgiastic frenzy. Paramedics pull the comatose bodies of those who have fainted out from the crowds, whisking them away on stretchers. Every shot is underscored by a feral screaming. A mullet-haired girl rips her soaked T-shirt from her body. The sweat-glazed arms of a young man reach out to the stage, the syllables of Michael's name stretching in a long, ecstatic wail. It's a perfect example of social contagion, how the emotional charge of group gatherings can elicit bizarre and intense behaviour. We see it in gigs and churches and football stadiums, this overspill of immense feeling that can tip into blissful euphoria or violent depravity.

As a piece of evidence in the case of Michael's impact, the video is hard to deny. I am them and they are me, feverish disciples at the altar of their one and only god. I've begun watching it compulsively. I want to want, my desire a forgone conclusion hunting for its subject. Michael was my first conduit and catalyst in this search. He matters immensely and not at all. I was a glass of feeling filled to the brim, constantly spilling out and over myself for lack of a large enough vessel. Michael was the largest and most brilliant that anyone could have. In all his strategic dazzle and magnitude, he was able to contain the diffuse longings of millions of people. But I loved him in a way that necessitated his distance, a distance both painful and blissfully safe. My love for Michael could take whatever shape it liked. I could choose which parts of him I engaged with and which I didn't. He was whoever I decided he was, whatever I needed him to be.

I would take the trite wisdom that we should never meet our heroes one step further and say we never do meet our heroes. The person we encounter in that unlikely instance is not the fantasy we have built in our heads. In the moment where the shapeless fantasy melds with the brute fact of a person, a private world is ruptured. This is one of many reasons I struggled to accept the idea of Michael's wrongdoing. It ruined the convenient fiction in my brain, one on which integral parts of myself had been built. In order to change the story of who Michael was to fit this new, disturbing reality, I would have to reassess my entire childhood, my way of thinking, my lofty aspirations of creative brilliance. What was left of me without these things? I didn't know, and for a long time I couldn't find the courage to find out.

* * *

At every Michael concert, a fan is picked to go on stage to greet Michael. These girls (and, yes, they are always girls) are not selected at random. Each fan is an instrument, selected to illustrate his greatness. It's entirely possible that every person chosen to join Michael on stage was sincerely overcome by their moment with Michael. But I wouldn't be surprised if there was a tacit audition process, where a shortlist of desperate fans would have to grovel and plead with Michael's honchos to prove how much they could ham up their display of adulation. As the Flagellants of the Middle Ages did when they whipped their own bodies in penitence, the fan pays what they believe is a worthy price for proximity to their deity. This dual intimacy and exposure, the clash of the personal and public, is a finely tuned string. In these moments, replicated in pretty much all of Michael's live shows, the spectacle of the fan running into his arms is disconcerting to watch. It's a moment of singular transcendence for the fan, who will experience nothing like this again, and a rote moment of status-building for Michael, who poses like a benevolent messiah as a parade of young girls crumble at his feet. I am mortified for them, yet still jealous. They have debased themselves, but who amongst us hasn't done so to please the object of our affections?

It reminds me of so much I've done as a girl to perform my desire in ways acceptable to the male ego, a set of overwrought gestures I have copied in the hope that some semblance of my feelings will register. Like all social conditioning, this doesn't always feel like an act, until you begin to ponder how we all arrived at the same flailing arms and howling throats. When our genuine desire and longing is forced into an outsized display, it's easy to perform to what's expected rather than what is felt. The moment of seeing your hero in the flesh might inspire a sharp spike of emotion, a cathartic release of suspense. But it is hardly ever the meeting of hearts or minds we might wish it to be. It is a photo op, a dinner party anecdote, a moment more satisfying in the recollection.

All the time, we offer sexual approximations of ourselves for money, safety and acceptance. We downplay how many professions are reliant on this charade, perhaps because of the ever-pervasive stigma around people who make this work plain. Sex workers know and understand the potency of intimacy, how it can be bartered and faked to convincing effect. The dynamic between pop star and rabid fan has strong parallels to the relationship between sex worker and client. In both instances, the dynamic is inherently lopsided. There can be no meaningful connection because of the wildly differing positions of power. Between a fan and their idol, neither party is entirely powerful or powerless. Both are tied up in a grisly symbiosis; neither can exist without the other. The relationship is heady, intoxicating, occasionally gratifying. It is also codependent, mutually destructive, fraught with resentments and the potential for grave violence. The two scenarios are certainly not equivalent, but I am struck by what they both teach us about desire when twisted by the demands of commerce.

I've always been fascinated by a certain type of man who frequents strip clubs, who wholly invests in and believes the convenient fantasy unfolding in front of him. It is possible, of course, to enjoy a spectacle while aware of its ultimate artifice. But we continually talk of a man's lust as so swift and blunt that he will either convince himself of the mutuality of the experience or force his desires onto the scenario. In his arrogance or ignorance this man may read the facade of fuck-me eyes on a pretty stripper as a genuine, unprecedented moment of erotic connection unmediated by money or power. We have rightfully analysed and critiqued how misogynist men bludgeon the personhood of women they desire, but we still don't seem to know how to discuss what is happening when the roles are reversed.

We have legislated the world around the pyre of men's uncontrollable horniness, yet comparable behaviour from women in response to the sexual displays of men is still considered inexplicable, a bizarre aberration that cannot be accounted for. It's difficult to compare these two scenarios without drowning in the murky waters of false equivalence. To be clear: I don't believe the objectification of men by straight women has ever been, or will ever be, as sinister, as constant or as deadly as the codified desires of straight men. But that doesn't mean that women don't have the capacity for a certain strain of entitlement to the famous men they make into vessels for their latent desire.

Mutual Need, Equal Risk

Every boy band I listened to as a teen sang songs about me. *You're the only one for me*, they crooned, close enough for it to tickle my ear, rouse the burgeoning yearn in my stomach. It sounded fun, driving a boy to complete distraction, his love so strong he'd perform a topless dance in the pouring rain with his mates, their outfits and harmonies synchronised. *I miss you, I want you, I want you back, back when I had you everything made sense.* A steady tumble of them piled up in the late nineties and early noughties, all matching outfits and bare torsos. Backstreet Boys, 5ive, Boyzone, *NSYNC, B2K, O-Town. Their songs were invitingly porous, vague enough for any young girl to insert herself as their subject. There is no specific narrative, no description of distinguishing features that might exclude me. I could imagine it was my hair, my eyes, my smile they sang of so passionately. Specificity is the death of seduction.

I wouldn't say I fancied these boys. Their baby faces and oiled pecs didn't yet ignite anything beyond mild satisfaction at their pleasing symmetry. My delight lay in what the ardent attention of a beautiful boy might confirm about me. Over the next few years, the beginnings of sexual intrigue would slowly emerge, and I would find myself drawn to the boys who were smiley and unthreatening, their eyes fringed with thick, feminine lashes.

I'm tickled by the subliminal wink in boy band names, the dog whistle you can only hear if tuned to the right frequency. Backstreet Boys. Take That. Boyzone. All hint at naughtier connotations: the backstreets in which one can get up to naughty things unseen by nosy authorities and disapproving parents; the private zones where boys initiate each other into manhood; the cheeky, boyish provocation to 'take that', 'that' being a punch, a shove, or something harder, more urgent.

At the peak of their popularity, boy bands' target demographics were (overtly) teenage girls and (covertly) gay men. For the latter, these bands were a rich trove of inadvertent homoerotica hiding in plain sight. The only popular boy band that were open about this were Take That, whose manager arranged for them to perform at gay clubs before they hit the big time. Their astonishing first music video for single 'Do

What U Like' shows them rubbing each other's naked torsos in jelly and cream, dressed in the leather garb of Soho muscle men. Years later, in the sepia-stained video for 'Pray', they pose in gestures combining the stately pomp of Greek statues and the femme stylings of voguers.

But the intersection of these worlds and their divergent messaging was invisible to me then: I was the fan who stood in the sun, a young girl who was widely understood as the target devotee. I was not literate in the subtle, cheeky ways that mainstream culture can be queered and vice versa. I was completely naive to the debt us straights owed, all the funk, groove and shimmy that grew in the petri dish of dance halls and discos. I shrink with shame at a vivid memory of me and a gaggle of friends gathered by the school computer, singing along to a parody of 'I Want It That Way' that instead asked 'Which Backstreet Boy Is Gay?' Once, as the tail end of 'Careless Whisper' played on the stereo, my Auntie told me that George Michael was 'one of those gays'. She shook her head, sighed, declared it 'such a waste'.

And though no member of the Backstreet Boys has come out as gay, in many of the boy bands of that time, it would transpire that at least one member was. It's no accident that most queer pop stars would only reveal this information long after they'd left the industry or were outed after their death. Being out and proud had consequences, could damage one's success in a pop market that flirted with subversion but ultimately served the status quo. This is perhaps why it was a compulsive pastime for us to speculate about these pretty yet inscrutable boys on our screens. It's sad enough that gay members of boy bands were forced to lie about who they were, directly or by omission. But was it about lying or more the sport of speculation? How to explain the glee we took in stripping away the facade, a facade that we both insisted on then took great pleasure in taking apart?

In the tell-tale annals of Google searches, our fixation with this still pulses – type the name of any male pop star and the second or third suggestion is sure to be that three-letter word, a word that is still, unbelievably, angled as an accusation.

Though we are said to live in slightly more permissive times, we are not far from the era when musicians, specifically squeaky-clean pop stars, had to feign singleness, availability and unambiguous straightness. Boy band members at the height of their youth, sex appeal and virility were not to publicly acknowledge any partners they may have and they certainly weren't to reveal a preference for their own gender. Vague rumours of dating other famous and beautiful women were okay, presumably because this maintained the image of their desirability but didn't threaten their one true commitment – that to their legion of young female fans.

K-pop is a fascinating case study in how far this orchestrated fantasy can stretch. In South Korea, heavily curated pop groups have been massively popular for over two decades. Only recently, thanks to the planet-shrinking powers of the internet, have K-pop groups reached a more international audience. This means the world has a glimpse into the seriousness of pop fandom in this culture. Bands like BTS and Tomorrow X Together have a po-faced discipline that makes their US and UK counterparts look like amateurs. Every aspect of their image, lifestyle, performance and music is created to prioritise the fan experience. It is not uncommon for the managers of these bands to assert a no-dating rule on band members. Relationships are corrosive to the obsequious world built for a largely young and female fan base who build an entire lifestyle around their favourite groups.

Then there's the subculture of homoerotic fantasy that a small but notable portion of young female fans have built. In a social media phenomenon labelled 'Larry Stylinson', a small cohort of One Direction superfans, known as Larries, created fan fiction and drawings centred on an imagined relationship between members Louis Tomlinson and Harry Styles. The theory that the two were in a passionate, secret love affair was not something shared with scorn or horror; rather, it was a portal through which these fans explored elliptical notions of intimacy and tenderness. I understand the succour a young girl finds in the thought of young men being soft, gentle and loving with each other, so few examples do they have of it elsewhere. For some, inserting themselves into this realm of desire as an active participant, even in the sphere of private fantasy, is daunting. Instead, here is something more thrilling, imbued with more urgency and longing: two boys desperately in love who must keep their bond secret. These girls take pleasure not in 'exposing' the truth but being its diligent guardians.

When the Larries came into public consciousness in a Channel 4 documentary about One Direction fans in 2013, some fans expressed sadness that this very specific and precious aspect of their world was cynically thrust into the spotlight with the veiled aim of mocking the girls who created it. Clearly, the cruel sport of 'exposing' people lives on, though we may now know better than to drag young men out of the closet for entertainment. There is another way of looking at this, of course. A cynic might call these fans sheltered and possessive, crafting disconcerting fictions that further objectify the boys they claim to care about. It also wouldn't be unfair to critique what could be seen as the fetishistic gaze of this fantasy. Arguably, these girls are unwanted interlopers who've wandered into the realm of male homoerotic love and somehow made it about them.

While boys have forever frustrated and disappointed me, I have also harboured a deep desire to know how they are amongst themselves. Unlike the derailing and intrusive fantasies so many men have of being amongst multiple women, I just wish to observe men in their tenderness, even if it is not directed towards me.

D'Angelo is naked on screen, or seemingly so. The shot ends as low on his hips as broadcast guidelines allow. It's clever. The mind lingers more on his cock because of this constant hint of it, more so than if we just saw it. It's there, undoubtedly, mere millimetres from where the camera's gaze cuts. Waiting. His body is a body whittled into discipline by many gym sessions, a dedicated personal trainer. It's clear he lifts heavy, faithfully eats his unseasoned chicken breast, could probably do several push-ups with a petite woman sat on the firm shelf of his back. And his skin, his skin exudes the warmth of polished wood. *How does it feel?* he asks us, and we watch as the camera makes its lecherous sweep around him. He swizzles slowly like a late-night kebab, but sexy, I suppose. *How does it feel?* he asks again. He really wants to know, curling his fists as he lets out an anguished wail of longing strong enough to wake James Brown from his grave.

D'Angelo was a consenting sex symbol. Seemingly so.

In 2000, D'Angelo set off on a tour for his album *Voodoo*, now widely considered one of the best cuts of R&B music ever recorded. A diligent musician who, like his idol Prince, was proficient on multiple instruments, D'Angelo took to song-writing with religious intensity. He studied the music of Jimi Hendrix, Roberta Flack and Joni Mitchell, obsessing over the sonic quality of different modes of analogue recording. With his band director Questlove, he developed a set that he believed to be a true testament to the power of live music. But running alongside this was the charged response to the music video for lead single 'Untitled (How Does It Feel)'. It ignited some restless charge in the women who watched it. They took leave of their senses, swooning, screaming, grabbing at any part of him they could reach. He enjoyed the attention, until he didn't any more.

D'Angelo is an undeniably beautiful man, but I've never been able to sit through the entire video. I'd love to say that's because I am above such blunt objectification, but my porn search history would suggest otherwise. No, my reluctance comes from the video's leaning towards a certain Mandingo aesthetic, with all the heavy cargo that comes with it. The oiled-up skin, the lingering close-ups on biceps and heaving torsos. It's a flattened form of black masculinity that shrill, sheltered white women in particular seem to lose their minds over. Of course, black women can be found aplenty amongst those willing to make meat of him, but the antebellum echoes ring a little strong for me to freely enjoy the spectacle, even with a heavy sprinkle of irony.

Lots of people loved that video, though. It catapulted

D'Angelo to new heights of fame. But as women throughout time could have told him for free, self-objectification is a pyrrhic bargain, one that proffers unearned trust in the public's ability to receive the nuance of a person. Once you've offered yourself up as a sex symbol, it invariably swallows any chance to deviate from or reject this version of yourself. You become one thing, at the cost of everything else. The video would come to be both boost and behemoth, crowning D'Angelo as the sex god of neo-soul. But he found himself positioned as a torso first and serious musician second by many of his fans. During tour dates, female audience members would scream at him to take his top off. His carefully curated set, his band of stellar musicians, all of it became secondary to his body and its assumed promises. This was at least part of the reason he withdrew from the spotlight for over a decade, claiming he couldn't wait to 'go in the woods, drink some hooch, grow a beard, and get fat'.

Though D'Angelo's brief taste of life as a sex object probably had some part to play in his long retreat from the music industry (it would be another fourteen years before he released the follow-up album to *Voodoo*), the fact remains that D'Angelo is still discussed largely in his capacity as a musician and singer. Most retrospectives on this era of his career focus on his talent, with his body and sex appeal serving as a footnote. Female musicians rarely get the same luxury. If gifted with the privilege and burden of conventional beauty, their talent invariably lives in the shadow of their image.

Britney's appearance was always placed front and centre of her mass appeal, and so the supposed 'loss' of her beauty, whether through weight gain or the spontaneous shaving of her head, became signs of her waning relevance. She was no longer fuckable to the men who once desired her or aspirational to the girls who wanted to be her. Without that, her cachet floundered. I remember watching her comeback performance on *The X Factor* in 2008. After two years away from music, during which she would regularly appear on the front pages of gossip magazines dishevelled and haunted-looking, this performance was framed as her chance to reclaim her pop star status. The pressure was on for Britney to prove that she was back on form, which meant a faithful copy of her late teen self. This despite the fact that by this time she was twenty-seven and the mother to two young boys. Ultimately, it was us fans who claimed to love her who demanded this. The public wanted Britney back and time-machine pretty, with no evidence that motherhood or the passage of time had changed her.

After being released from her conservatorship in 2021, one of many ways Britney chose to celebrate was taking and posting nude pictures of herself on Instagram. The pictures are blurry and often awkwardly posed. She twists her body towards the camera, one arm shielding her breasts. Her hair is tied in a hasty ponytail; dark circles frame her eyes. The shots are slightly bizarre and try hard, yet still somehow self-possessed. It's the frank nudity of a woman in her forties finally free to make her own mistakes. I'd wager that people's response of detached bemusement is better than the hungry gaze of lecherous men and impressionable young girls looking for how and when and if their bodies should be, and for whom.

Former boy band members from across the decades all have similar, harrowing stories of their young, female fans. In his autobiography *Moonwalk*, Michael describes his experience in the days of The Jackson 5:

> Being mobbed by near hysterical girls was one of the most terrifying experiences for me in those days . . . the fans would find out we were there and demolish the place, just tear it up . . . Those girls were serious. They still are. They don't realise they might hurt you because they're acting out of love. They mean well, but I can testify that it hurts to be mobbed. You feel as if you're going to suffocate or be dismembered. There are a thousand hands grabbing at you. One girl is twisting your wrist this way while another girl is pulling your watch off. They grab your hair and pull it hard, and it hurts like fire.

When Berry Gordy signed The Jackson 5 to Motown in 1968 he promised to make them a sensation – the black equivalent of The Beatles. After a heady trio of hits in the form of 'I Want You Back', 'ABC' and 'The Love You Save', Gordy's prophecy came good. Much like The Beatles, the crowds at their gigs were mostly made up of teenage girls who were often as taken by the fantasy of relationships with the boys as they were by the catchy tunes they played. It's a complex bind: these bands would not have enjoyed anything near the success they had if their largely female fans had not been so passionate and loyal. Yet everything spilled way past the bounds of propriety. Sometimes, they screamed so loud at the gigs that they drowned out the band. The tactics of superfans desperate for a glimpse of their favourite stars were wild and numerous. They would break into hotels and even private homes, mob department stores and concoct tall tales of secret relationships and pregnancies.

Little wonder, then, that some of Michael's biggest hits feature conniving women relentless in their pursuit of sexual power. Billie Jean claims to be pregnant with his child. Diana strategically coerces him into her web. He was hyper-aware of the shadow of sex and how it played out from his childhood. He witnessed the advantage his brothers took of an endless supply of adoring girls, sometimes having sex in the hotel rooms the brothers would share. Michael would lie in his bed, inevitably hearing everything. Even their father was rumoured to sleep with young fans while on the road. Michael was a child privy to sexual behaviour he hadn't the maturity or wherewithal to process. There was also the paranoia that comes with knowing that at any moment you could be swamped by a mob of girls so desperate to have a piece of you that they are willing to tear you apart to get it. Later in his autobiography, Michael solemnly and ironically stated that 'when sex is used as a form of blackmail or power, it's a repugnant use of one of god's gifts'.

When reading studies on the potentially negative effects of early initiations into sex, it's clear that any neat conclusions on what causes inappropriate behaviour in later life are impossible to draw. Measuring cause and effect when it comes to human sexual behaviour is complicated for a plethora of reasons. Trying to distinguish what circumstances have more influence over others is tricky. Is poverty, mental illness, early abuse and neglect or poor education more likely to tip the balance? The data has no clear answers. Assessment of sexual behaviour also relies on testimony from the people studied, and humans tend to struggle in accurately and honestly self-reporting their feelings and motivations. There are a handful of convincing extrapolations from the data at hand, such as a 2015 study that suggests that early exposure to sexual activity has negative effects on a young adult's health. But it's important to stress that such studies are not resounding in their findings, which makes analysis difficult but, in my opinion, still worthwhile.

That said, these subsequent thoughts are necessarily speculative, based on trying to put myself in the shoes of a child dropped into a situation like Michael's. It strikes me that most of us would struggle to develop a functional notion of sex in such insane circumstances. What does a child learn as they observe these excesses of violent passion, with no context or apparent safeguards? Does your body ever feel like your own when it's been pushed, pulled and pawed by thousands of rabid fans? How to process all the mixed feelings, the intrigue, the fear, the disgust? A pop star of any stature has to reckon with their own sexualisation, which in the demands of our sex-obsessed world is non-negotiable. For many men who come of age under the spotlight, acting on this currency has been both a fringe benefit and potential sledgehammer to success. We can see how dangerous it is to learn your first lessons about sex in such a distorted environment, where you are treated as both an expendable object and a god entitled to the body of whomever you please. It would take an unusual well of integrity or circle of even-keeled loved ones to hold you to task. This leaves a little too much to happenstance in the harsh vacuum of fame, with its queasy combination of paranoia and entitlement.

This is the point where I might demonstrate my personal stake in all this. Writerly conventions dictate that at this juncture there ought to be some reveal, the inciting incident of my own horrific assault, perhaps. I have none to offer. By some arbitrary stroke of luck, I have reached this point in my life unmolested and unraped. Other than the gropings every girl on this earth must endure, instances too wearisome and boring to list, I am so far unscathed. I used to live in constant, low-level fear of it. This may seem needlessly alarmist, but I was merely taking my cues from the world around me, the stench of sexual trauma that clung to so many women I knew, my favourite books from the library. There it was in *The Color Purple*, *The Lovely Bones* and again in *The Bluest Eye*. It seemed to be a matter of if, not when, this grisly rite of passage would occur.

But even so, I've been dogged by the threat. Once, aged ten, I was sat in a dentist's waiting room when a much older man, forgoing all the empty seats to sit right next to me, pressed his thigh against mine. Heart thwacking against my chest, I moved to a seat squarely in the receptionist's eye line as his eyes remained on me until my mother came back from the toilets. I have gone home with men who handled my body with a carelessness bordering on but never quite tipping into violence. Other times I have laid passive and let things I'd rather not happen happen, quietly astonished that my muted participation did nothing to pull the man from his eyeless, private world of lust. Sex has been good, sometimes, and it has also been lowly and lonely. And in this, I am lucky compared to many.

Our first handful of intimate encounters follow us into adult life and form the template of our expectations. The persistent trend of coercion, both its harm and its troubling erotic potential, has seeped through all aspects of our sexual psyche. Even in our burgeoning consent-focused culture, we struggle to invent new ways of initiating, thinking and speaking about sex that aren't mired by this old script.

The hope is that our intimate lives might be a refuge from all that is cruel and vicious about the world. But all those complex, ugly feelings that slosh around inside us find their way into how we share our bodies with or force our bodies on other people. But the uber-fans amongst us enter a double bind of risk when we fall in love with famous strangers. Our desire may become so feral and self-seeking that we swallow our heroes whole, or that same desire may be used against us. A clamouring fan can be plucked from the crowd, assumed to be willing and hungry. It's true: we can crave the affections of those who hurt us, feel honoured for being *chosen*. Why do we insist on the lie that to be a victim is to exist only in fear and hurt? The complicated truth is that, like all relationships, the dynamic between ardent fan and opportunist star is layered, the gristle of threat marbled with the sinew of want. This is one reason of many that victims struggle to name what happened to them, can spend years in denial of their own subjugation. What about the moments that I thrilled at the attention, a fan might ask themselves, drowning in unearned guilt. What about the moments I stood in the crowd, screaming their name?

⋆

I have long felt like a fraudulent straight person. It's a suit that has never fitted right – too tight in some places and hopelessly baggy in others. I've never managed to find ways into it that didn't require, in some way, my intellectual or physical debasement. A mutual meeting of minds and crotches would be delightful. Honest filth and unquestioned respect is the aim, the electric play between feminine and masculine without assigning anyone's roles too firmly. That's what I'd love, please and thank you. But this has eluded me for so long that my deductive brain accepts that what I want is something of a mirage, a theorist's wet dream.

I am weary of the rules and regulations of straightness, insulted by the contortions that make a woman pleasing to a critical mass of men. I consider the whole thing a vicious scam with ever-diminishing returns. Perhaps I'm too enamoured by my own misandry, which I'll admit has a strange, self-defeating eroticism all its own. It feels both woeful and righteous to refuse men as sexual and romantic partners. What might seem defeatist to others to me feels rather thrilling in its active thrust. *No* is a muscle after all, and I've become adept at flexing it.

And so for now I don't date, I don't fuck, I flirt for fun to remind myself I can, but no more. This facade fits snug as a second skin, underneath it is the pesky wistfulness I cannot shake. I don't think I would mind it all so much, this abstinence, if I felt the stakes weren't so stacked against me as the woman-shaped thing, the hole, the one who must always acquiesce with *okay* and *fine* and *yes*. My truth is that I often feel there is no real love or respite to be found between me and another man, not really, at least not a man committed to masculinity at its most rigid and rote, faithful to the script we keep calling love for lack of imagination. The shadow of all these disappointments is so very long and the attempts to create something unsaddled by this so tiring and circuitous, especially as most straight men have no desire or incentive to do this work at all.

In her essay 'My Mixed Marriage', the American essayist, poet, novelist and comic-book writer Dodie Bellamy talks about her marriage with poet Kevin Killian, who self-defined as a gay man. Rather than a feeling of mismatched desire, she describes a feeling of 'mutual need and equal risk' with her partner, one that eluded her with other men she had been with. I feel a surge of longing when I read these words. It's what I've felt the profound lack of in so many of my attempts at romantic connection.

Perhaps what I lament is that queer love and relationships, by necessity, have been able to create their own terms in deviation from social norms. Though it's a profound advantage to love and fuck in ways that society doesn't demonise, this means that us supposed normals are not encouraged to ask ourselves: what is this? What are the specific and considered ways in which we could love each other? What are the specific, considered things about this dynamic that might cause unintentional pain? Though living in a world that forces some to define themselves in contrast to a fixed standard is demeaning, it at least allows the potential for something chosen, a praxis of love and sex assembled with intention and not a small amount of defiance.

Diana Ross was Michael's first love, a woman he described as being like a mother, sister and lover all at once. Diana, eyes forever wide in disbelief, twiggy limbs dwarfed by that big, black storm cloud of hair. Everything about her both elevated and mocked the bird-like femininity she exuded. Like a drag queen with his muse, Michael's draw to her was part maternal, part romantic. As with all mama's boys, there is something of the Oedipal lingering beneath, too.

Diana Ross is one of many beautiful women Michael collected over the years. Like jewels arranged side by side in a velvet case, they sparkle: Elizabeth Taylor, Brooke Shields, Tatum O' Neal, Katharine Hepburn. These women all share the classic, hyperfeminine beauty of a bygone era. Each have their delicate features, their large eyes and skin white as a brisk, winter sky.

In the nineties, Michael cast supermodels Iman and Naomi Campbell in the videos for 'Remember The Time' and 'In The Closet' respectively. The signalling of lust is more overt than in his early videos, where the most he did was wrap his leading ladies in an anaemic embrace. But it was a new dawn, with Madonna wiggling her Jean Paul Gaultier tits and hip hop bursting onto the mainstream, with its braggadocious lyrics and half-naked honeys. Michael had to show his hand in this emerging era of sexual explicitness.

If you've seen the sterile kisses between co-stars in old Hays Code-era Hollywood movies, you've a good visual reference for how devoid of passion the kiss between Michael and Iman is in the 'Remember The Time' video. It's like what two kids might do in the park while their parents' backs are turned, an experiment borne of clinical rather than carnal intrigue. They awkwardly mash faces, their lips barely meeting. Iman's neck cranes under the weight of her crowned head as she kneels in slow motion, slowly slipping out of Michael's arms. It is supposed to be the narrative apex of the video, but instead it reads like an ironic reversal of accelerating desire.

For 'In The Closet', Michael recruited Herb Ritts to direct and Naomi Campbell to star as his love interest. Ritts specialised in videos and photos that worked with shadow and light to emphasise the contours of his models' angular faces and statuesque bodies. In other words, he made striking images of unusually hot people. In the video, Michael and Naomi Campbell gyrate near, rather than on, each other. Naomi's sleepy eyes try their best to evoke sexual tension. Michael wears a dirty wife beater and black jeans in what I assume is an attempt at earthy ruggedness that no one has ever associated with or required of him.

Both these videos read to me as exercises in desperate hetero-theatre. But most bizarre of all is that we demand these displays of legible, instructive desire from our pop stars at all.

Michael, perhaps, is the first gay boy I ever loved. Gay in the sense that he transcended (or failed, depending on who you ask) conventional forms of manliness. Gay in the sense that he loved women but also seemed terrified of them. Gay in the sense that people assumed he was gay. Any gestures he made to disprove this never felt plausible. He performed heterosexuality in a way that only a parodist can – the cartoon pelvic thrust of someone who has watched and mimicked, rather than felt the animal impulse these movements signal.

Michael kept gorgeous, high-status women on his arm to not only signal a heterosexuality and masculinity that the world expected of him, but perhaps also because he yearned to be near a beauty he believed he didn't possess. If a beautiful woman chooses to give you her time and affection, agrees to be seen with you, it demonstrates your worthiness to the rest of the world. But the initial thrill of this proximity cannot last. The closer one is to the beauty of others, the more isolated and grotesque you feel in comparison. Eventually, your own lack feels ever more apparent and shameful. You cannot cheat your way to a feeling, no matter how much you surround yourself with its markers.

Socially sanctioned beauty is not just about who has more currency in sex and relationships, but who does or doesn't get hired, how likely we are to be believed as a figure of authority or in a court of law. In short, desire obfuscates our judgement. We are softened by our primary response to an aesthetically pleasing face. *This is good! This is safe! This is sacred!* our mammalian brains tell us. While it's entirely possible for desire and fear to coincide, especially when we realise that we cannot possess or control the object of our desire, it is also true that our desire for a person can be a gauze over our eyes and conscience.

Here's the irony about beauty, as defined in its most stringent and unforgiving terms: I suspect we all feel excluded from it, regardless of where we fall on the beauty scale. I learnt early, thank god, that the model-esque girls I envied and resented in my youth were usually no happier in their skin than their 'average' counterparts. My beef was never with them, but with the rules none of us had set and that all of us were failed by. The attention and favourable treatment the beautiful receive, much like fame, does little to dent the questions we must all ask ourselves of who we are and who might love us in our messy entirety.

⋆

I am nine years old and playing hairdresser, fucking around with a blunt pair of scissors. As you can guess, this story doesn't end well. The result was a ragged clash of lengths, errant tufts sticking out every which way, each angle unfortunate. The cut was irresolvable. My mother arrived home and flipped when she saw what I'd done.

It's a chilling sound, the dull buzz of clippers. I'd always dreaded Sundays when I sat through having my hair blow-dried and twisted into tight cornrows. But as the clipper razed its way across my scalp, it didn't hurt anywhere near as much as that weekly tug and ache. I cried then with a different pain, the pain of vanity and the looming punishment of ugliness. In Uganda, it's not uncommon for parents to shave their daughters' heads. This is part practicality, part deferral of the looming pageantry of womanhood. But I did not live in Uganda. I lived in the UK, where school was a scatter of Rosies and Poppys and Taras whose hair tickled their backs. The young black girls on relaxer boxes had hair that swished and shone. Mine was gone.

At this juncture in time, McDonald's would include toys in their Happy Meals, one for girls and one for boys. McDonald's was Mecca. I loved its too-bright lights and the view of the fryers behind the counter, bubbling with oil. The tiny vials of ketchup also pleased me, as did a salty fry chased with a straw-pull on a large vanilla milkshake. The staff member handed the box to my Uncle, who handed it to me. The outside displayed a scene of go-karts and checkered flags. I had been assigned a label, the wrong one. I think I remember crying, if not in the McDonald's, then in Uncle's car.

Uncle assured me they must have confused my Happy Meal with another child's. It was a kind lie. He wiped my cheeks with the pad of his flat, dry thumb. It's this I recalled when I first had to get my head around the notion of gender dysphoria – the profound hurt and dissonance of how you feel inside being illegible to others. In a last-ditch attempt to cheer me up, Uncle told me I looked like one of the most glamorous women in the world. I wrinkled my nose at the name. It didn't spark any recognition.

Grace Jones?

Who on earth was Grace Jones?

When I saw a picture of Grace Jones for the first time, I was terrified. Everything about her threw me off balance. Her solid block of hair. The frank, sometimes bulging eyes and obsidian skin. She did not smile. She bared her teeth. Her body yielded no softness, just lines and corners. I was embarrassed by how willingly she posed in a cage, naked on all fours, for her French white lover. The label above the cage read 'DO NOT FEED THE ANIMAL'. Is that what we were? Animals? Young and desperately preoccupied with being 'correct' at femininity, I didn't understand why Grace Jones revelled so much in flouting the rules of prettiness. Why did it seem so dangerous? Why did it seem, treacherously, like fun?

Later I would learn about the era which birthed Grace and she began to make more sense. The eighties was a time of angles. Its synth sounds were spiky and impatient, its economy plunging, soaring, then plunging again. Angry red blusher sliced through cheeks like a wound and everyone's hair crunched with the thick defence of hairspray. Grace Jones along with Boy George, Annie Lennox and Prince were poster figures for an era of emerging androgyny, eliciting equal parts fascination and unease.

After Grace, came Nina. On hearing her voice, I was immediately troubled. My first question was 'Is that a man or a woman?' I did not like what I heard, not yet. Making categorical sense of that sound was the only way I had to control the complicated feelings her voice aroused in me. I was pulled by intrigue, pushed by suspicion. Nothing about Simone's voice, face or politics was inviting or concessionary. Like Grace, she eschewed easy femininity. Even her songs that flirted with pretty, tinkly melodies were troubled by her dark and unlovely voice, its beautiful ironies and heavy weariness. No matter what heights it scaled, it always seemed to land in a trough, even when her songs celebrated freedom, love, the welcome arrival of the sun. Like red wine, I had to acquire the taste for it, listening again and again until the shadows in the music felt less like foreboding and more like home. Who said home is always comfortable or always safe? It is merely the place that feels familiar, that knows you in all your disrepair.

In my family, there was always an unquestioned respect for Michael's weirdness. If we ever mocked him, it was in the genial way that family members tease each other. But he was one of ours, no matter how odd he looked or behaved. We happily made concessions to the things about him that confused and disturbed us. The rules that applied to the rest of us did not apply to him. He wasn't black, he wasn't white, not a man nor a woman. Even 'human', for better and for worse, did not seem a fitting category for him. He was Michael, another thing entirely, more of an experience than a person.

But, for many, Michael's blackness mattered and his femininity stood in direct conflict with his race. When you belong to a culture that already sits on the periphery, gender performance has different stakes. The fear around nonconformity in the black community is a complex issue. Respectability politics plays its role, as does a certain conservatism borne from the Christian faith many of us are brought up in. Though I begrudge no one their religious beliefs, it's frustrating when Christianity is treated as intrinsic to black identity. Its roots in our diaspora were embedded by colonial powers. This biblical god was forced on us, filtered through those who cared more about our compliance than our salvation. When this same god is evoked to shame us for failing at gender and all its airless pageantry, I feel maddened and so very, very bored.

Michael's particular brand of gender ambiguity did not read as defiant. He didn't have the cheeky decisiveness that Grace had, who seemed to delight in how her presentation hinted at queerness and deviance. Still, Michael's soft, high voice, pancaked face and long black hair were read as womanly. Newspapers printed rumours that he was undergoing what was then called a sex change.

These stories reportedly mortified Michael. This was not a grey area that he wanted to court. At the time, he still belonged to the Jehovah's Witness faith that he'd grown up with. According to their doctrine, being gay is an abominable sin. He wasn't long out of Motown's crucible, a place that groomed its black artists to represent and appease traditional, Middle American values. Despite what was then his fairly clean, family-friendly image, Michael's androgynous appearance was brought up in conservative media outlets as a bad influence on young people. Reading these newspaper clippings, it's noteworthy how brief these cycles of gender panic are. For every generation, this conversation seems fresh and uncharted, yet our media archives show us that while the language we use may change, these needless anxieties are nothing new.

The suspicion and disappointment around Michael's appearance amongst certain black people was touched on by cultural critic Nelson George. In an eyebrow-raising essay about the star, he wrote: 'Michael Jackson's nose job, often ill-conceived makeup, and artificially curled hair is, in the eyes of many blacks, a denial of his color that constitutes an act of racial treason. Add to that a disquieting androgyny and you have an alarmingly un-black, unmasculine figure as the most popular black man in America.'

In watching Michael be both revered and reviled this way, a young black boy learns harsh lessons about the consequences of indulging his not-quite-ness. If he is forthright enough, he might decide that alienation from his community is a worthwhile price for freedom of expression. But fame is not an available shield for the mere mortal who cannot lean on talent and riches to soften the blow of ridicule.

Michael was neither the first nor the last singer to be handed this heavy mantle of representation, but the magnitude of his fame no doubt amplified the pressure he was under. The imperative of 'good' masculinity for black men has many things teeming under its surface. It is both a reaction to historical disempowerment and a redemptive tale of reclaimed dignity. It's a strict ideal, one that has no doubt robbed countless black men of their full humanity. When even the King of Pop cannot fully escape these strictures, it shows how punishing these expectations are.

Ambiguity is something I now seek out, the hinterland where I believe all truly beautiful things live. I used to wish that nine-year-old me had known the long precedent there was for her bald little head. I'm glad now of the ignorance I had and the unease I felt. It was necessary. In that pit of assumed 'wrongness', I learnt who I might be without the crutch of pretty. From there it was difficult, but possible, to invent more interesting versions of myself. Freedom from conformity is something I have to keep choosing, even when it is lonely and frightening. Those who have this need, and take this risk, are out there. We look for each other in crowds, hear each other in certain songs. We gather close, knowing we can at least be lonely and frightened together.

You'd Never Do That To Me

'Who's this?' I asked Auntie. In my hand, a photo of her. In it, she is older than I was then, yet young, younger than she'd been and younger than I am now. So much hair! It was long, hot-combed stiff and past her shoulders. Her cheekbones sat high and proud as they still did then, and now, under their new cover of softer skin and liver spots. The Auntie I visited worried about her teeth, never had juice or fizzy drinks in the fridge. Young Auntie in the photo is unrepentant, a bottle of Coca-Cola in her hand.

But I had seen many pictures of Auntie from before I was born. That alone was not what bothered and thrilled me. I pointed at the man next to her, whom I didn't recognise.

Auntie, normally so compliant when I asked my busybody questions, suddenly found herself urgent tasks in the kitchen. Opening a cupboard, then shutting it, swiping a cloth along an already clean counter. 'Where did you find that?' she asked, an edge to her usually gentle voice. Snooping was a compulsive hobby of mine. What else was I to do in those long summers with all their cruel idle hours? I had no business rifling through her things, but in my defence, I'd been looking for the fancy set of pencils I knew she kept in some drawer or other. The search reaped no pencils, but I did find a picture of her and a strange man tucked amongst her personal effects.

There were always photos floating around, portals to a time and place foreign to me. Firmly past the threshold of double digits, I had a body and mind brushing against their own limits, desperate for things just out of reach. This was the time for poking into shadowy corners of family lore, stomping my boots through the loaded silences of grown-ups.

I had sensed a story, a crucial one. Her furtive response proved me right.

Auntie lifted a cup of tea to her lips and sipped. Finally, she said, 'He was someone I was very fond of back home.' She tilted her head from side to side, seemed to swill the words around her mouth.

'He was . . . a very good friend.'

I wasn't having that. Her resistance was a hard scab I was desperate to peel back.

'So he was your boyfriend?' I pressed, having only recently grasped the weight of this word, how it could leave a crater in a conversation. I had only the woolliest notions of what a boyfriend actually was or did.

Auntie shook her head. 'Boyfriend? No. That wasn't what we called it.'

'Then what was it?'

'We just spent a lot of time together in my college days. 'He,' she paused, then carefully said, 'he took care of me.'

'So he was your boyfriend?' I persisted.

'Why are you asking?'

'He's looking at you like he loves you.' I may even have arched my eyebrow as I said this, wielding a worldliness I hadn't earned.

Auntie snorted. 'What do you know about that?' But she was smiling a smile I'd never seen before. For a moment, she became the girl in the picture, bright-eyed, tightly coiled, learning her own mischief.

The man's body stretches across the long grey sofa, his legs splayed. His left arm is slung across the back of the sofa, a large hand hovering close to, but not touching, Auntie's neck. The hairs on my own raise looking at it. The photo is living. Auntie looks into the lens, but he looks right at her, as if she's a riddle he's on the cusp of solving.

She gave me scant pieces of information. His name was Jerry. Okay. They met at a party. Whose party? A cousin, Brenda. You remember Auntie Brenda, she says, and I do. She wore shiny, synthetic wigs and was, apparently, a wild child by a particular Ugandan measure. The bane of the family, Auntie's favourite person in the world. Despite this, she almost didn't go. Brenda had convinced her, done her hair with the hot comb that all six women in the house had to share. As they walked in together, Auntie saw him. He was holding court on the verandah. His nostrils, she said, were mesmerising. They flared when he laughed. Jerry was a professor at the local university, handsome, tall, well-read. He didn't put on a fake British accent or reject local attire like most Ugandan men of his stature. 'He was unlike a lot of men I knew,' she told me, now completely warmed up. 'He liked listening to what I had to say.'

She is looking at the photo as if she wants to dive into it. I feel like an intruder, my hasty footprints all over her memories.

I would come back to the story in increments. Later, as a teenager, I would notice how very young she looks in the picture, how Jerry's face hints at jowls.

'How old was he?'

Auntie shifted in her seat. 'I don't remember,' she said at first. Then: 'He never told me.' I waited. She closed her eyes, tilted her head up to the ceiling, calculating. 'I think he must have been at least forty-five, maybe older.'

'How old were you?'

'Fifteen.'

I struggled through the maths, adding five to my age, considering how old my mother was. Anything over the age of twenty felt ancient. Forty-five, sixty-five and seventy-four were barely distinguishable from each other, all lumped into the firm category of 'old'.

There were things I didn't pick up on then, threads that I would weave into this story over many years. Some came from Auntie, others from my own sleuthing and imaginative summations. Jerry was married with four children. Auntie had known and accepted this from the very beginning. It was normal then, and in some cultures and contexts still is. When her parents couldn't afford it, he stepped in and paid her school fees until she was eighteen. He supported her pursuit of academia, even when parents and friends discouraged her from getting a degree. They lost touch after she graduated, but it wasn't her who let their tether fray. Jerry was the one who withdrew and eventually stopped returning her calls. She later learnt that his youngest child had grown sick with malaria and died. He was only three years younger than her. Not long after, she met Uncle, a friend of her brother's, a man her family knew and approved of. Jerry passed away a year after Auntie and Uncle moved to the UK. Rumours found their way to Auntie even then: Jerry had died from AIDS and given it to his wife who was miraculously still alive. All of this happened before Auntie turned twenty.

Maybe she loved him, in that vertiginous way that's only possible at that age. I would come to know it, too, at sixteen and twenty-six and still, exhaustingly at thirty: the flood of gratitude when a commanding man turns his precious attention, that he could aim anywhere, towards you. But it is never enough. In the end, it proves itself a fickle honour. Your whole young life can pass in that dim glow, only for a shard of something else to slice through the idyll. One wrong comment, and the way they look at you changes. You are no longer the shiny trinket you once were. You become dumb as a bluebottle banging against the pane of an open window. What use is the world when the man that handed you your confidence no longer wants you?

Auntie would field my questions about Jerry for many years. The story taunted me as I kept pushing at its pressure points. Now, my knotted hypothesis is this: Auntie's first love was an older, married man. He believed he loved her, too, but more likely he enjoyed his outsize impression on her. There was, no doubt, a submerged respect for her mind. I imagine it felt good for Auntie to be listened to by such a respected man, to have her emerging opinions taken seriously. But what about the disregard for his family, the young girls who he aimed for? I doubt that Auntie was the only one. What about the panning for young skin and eyes untroubled by jadedness. And why not? It was the way of his father and his father before him, and almost all the men around them. Why would you do the right or better thing when everywhere people do largely as they please?

Did Auntie sometimes wonder if any struggles she lived with later in life were her comeuppance for fucking someone else's husband? I knew they considered me an honorary daughter, but I sometimes wondered why they never had any of their own. Did she chalk this up to retribution for that other woman's pain, the children who she chose not to think about when she spent those stolen nights with him? It's hard to reckon with our tallies, let alone keep count of other people's. Did Jerry look back on the affair as a footnote in his complicated life? Did he feel or consider his power and how brazenly he abused it, or did he, like most of us, feel more in tune with all that eluded him, the desperate need to be a man as defined by other men?

He is facing away from you, but the muscles of his back greet you through his shirt. You are backlit like a Barry Jenkins film, the moon perving on the two of you through the curtains. The rent is paid, your underwear obedient, screw-top wine has you just the right side of tipsy. You possess the mysticism of Erykah Badu and the bionic thighs of Serena Williams, on which you most certainly intend to let him lay his pretty head. Evidence of a well-spent evening is strewn across the room: scented candles, scattered Rizlas, a jumper slipped off as the heating thawed the room. Both of you are acting a bit, but it doesn't feel oppressive. It's nice to have someone to pretend for, baby hairs behaving, stomachs sucked in, bedroom tidied and anecdotes dusted free of hazards.

His fingers brush through the stack of vinyl on the wall and you shake your head in private satisfaction. Look at you and this lickable intellectual. His skin matches yours when you hold his forearm against your own. India Arie sang about this seamlessness, your pengness affirming his in a gorgeous feedback loop.

He holds aloft another record. This one has a shirtless black man wonkily smirking on the front. 'What about this next?' he says, his mouth breaking into a boyish grin as you nod your approval. Al Green does his thing as you think how Kanye was right about slow jams, the plaintive, simmering effect of the songs we inherited from our parents. You ponder the political miracle of this music, all the places and spaces it occupies. How it somehow transcended the pungent blackness of the people singing it and became the universal soundtrack of yearning.

He approaches you like a man who knows the power of a slow and considered approach. You are draped in shadow and heavy musk. The moment is perfect, his lips make a beeline for yours, but your brain suddenly recalls: wasn't it Al Green who once beat his wife with a shoe for refusing to do what you're about to do with each other? You remember reading it on Wikipedia, you tell him. He is nonplussed, and so are you. Why have you brought this up?

Because you're in the habit of scanning the biography of every soul artist you love, looking for reasons to hurt and seethe. And isn't it remarkable, you continue, as your date exhales and takes himself to the sofa, that the coo of Al Green's voice in 'You Are So Beautiful' is the diametric opposite to that image? How can those two things exist in the same body? Close your eyes and picture it, you instruct him, and he does, his cock probably softening in his jeans, his hand itching to reach for his phone. How can someone who sings like that do something like this? He shrugs, as if this is a rhetorical question, but the thing is, you want a clear, straight answer, and his bemused face is nothing short of cowardly and ruinous.

Now you think about it, there is a callousness in the set of his shoulders. You can see how the boredom in his eyes might flicker into malice. Yes, yes, it's very clear to you now how these things hide in the tiny gestures and Freudian slips. You don't even know this man's second name, what his exes think of him, whether he double-locked the door after you walked in. You are doing the thing again, but you can't stop. It is comforting, laying out the worst-case scenarios, the potential worst of every man. You won't be the chump who sits in shock after the fact, disbelief stumbling from your lips: *I had no idea. I had no idea he was capable of something like this.*

You wonder if Al and Teddy and Sam and Otis fucked their lovers to their own music, bringing demo tapes from the studio and slipping them inside the deck as they poured themselves a measure of something smooth and brown. But who wouldn't, looking like that, sounding like that? Wouldn't you? you ask him, not appreciating the long sigh that rushes from his mouth. You want him to list every questionable thing he's ever done, lay it out on a chronological timeline for you to assess. You look over at his shoe rack in the corridor, a neat row of trainers, dress shoes and loafers. With enough gusto in the throw, they could cause damage, split a brow, leave a yellow if not purple bruise. You've often thought of how the sheer fact of darker skin minimises the violence, how cuts and scars do not contrast as sharply as they do on white skin.

He is offering you another drink and a change in subject. He is talking about singing voices and who has the best one, and it strikes you how much you enjoy this, the softness of his umms and the gentle proffering of *d'you-know-what-I-means* at the end of his sentences. The thing you like most is how a man sounds in the canal of your ear where it tickles. You like that Barry White sounds like an oak barrel and Al Green is a pleading bird with its chest puffed out.

You have to applaud his game because he's managed to back up out of this cul-de-sac of battered wives and back into safe, rollicking roads of nostalgia. Relief: songs you remember from your school days. The brown boys of the early noughties, Pretty Ricky, Bobby Valentino and Mario. You have not googled them and so you feel safe to remember the music and chuckle at the zigzag cornrows and earnest body rolls of the era. He has his hand on your knee, and then it's beginning, the way he rests his mouth in your collarbone and breathes, the quickening Tetris of legs.

You wonder if, like so many, these men made love more passionately through the promises they made than they ever did with their bodies. How on earth can you fuck better than how Marvin Gaye's 'I Want You' sounds? It teases a satiation just shy of human experience. It is desire incarnate, and desire necessarily wilts in the face of its object.

The fact of the matter is you've chased a moment that does good on the promise of this music. And sometimes, in some brief snatches across your life, you have felt it, the reason why Marvin screamed and Minnie Riperton whistled. And yet the quiet tragedy is that the act so rarely does justice to the music that serves it. On a record, the grooves are familiar and the climax promised. It comes when bidden and never overstays its welcome. It never forces itself where it's not wanted, it stops with the press of a button, a flick of a switch.

In the lead-up to nights like this, you have made playlists of black people singing about love and sex. In the absence of confidence you have stolen theirs. Here, you tell the flighty purr of Janet Jackson, I entrust you with this awkward British body, all its inexperience and occasional waves of grandeur. The songs play in strict sequence, like an incantation. It works, thank fuck, every time. You were embarrassed before, by the Poundland flimsiness of your own wanting. It seemed to lack focus, always crumbled on contact. The music taught you how to fake the wanting. You fondly recall each time the music induced something pretty close to the real thing.

You think of the churches these black singers often run back to, renouncing the secular music world to become pastors. The pulpit returns to them as a sanctuary, though these same churches often turned them away. Here, they learn that famished growl from the altar and use it in songs that worship the hallelujah of a woman's hips. The church shunned what it birthed: R&B, hip hop, crucifix-wearing womanisers, closeted men who sang songs to a phantom 'she' until their dying day and men who were no freer outside of those closets, so squeezed were they into the stifled dark of their own minds.

You are drunk now, and when you are drunk you allow yourself to listen to Michael. You sigh with joy at the opening drums of 'Rock With You', surely one of the best love songs of all time. A memory bubbles up to the surface, of your Auntie and Uncle swaying together in the living room. You used to watch them and think that was it, that was what love as an action is. Swaying with your eyes closed, holding each other up. You do what you hope reads as come-hither circles with your hips. You want to dance with this beautiful man, but he shakes his head. Shy. But after a couple more beckons he's up, wrapping his arms around your waist and swaying with you, rocking with you. You whisper a potted history of the song in his ear, how the writer of the song, Rod Temperton, said Michael was more comfortable singing songs about partying than parties themselves. This is the magic of a Michael Jackson love song. They are so moving, so believable, because they were sung in the valley between loneliness and imagination, the desperation of one feeding the other.

You are slurring your words now. His grip on your waist is loosening. Did you know, you say, that the original demo was more up-tempo but Quincy Jones smoothed it out, made it sound like the inside of a conch shell. Those were Michael's words, about the conch shell. Did you know that? you ask. He did not. He is sitting back down again, checking his phone. You have exhausted the night, his patience. Best to get on with the promised act.

After, he lands distracted kisses across your shoulders as you lie on your side in what you hope is a pleasing shape. You think about how you have floated on top of many moments like this, surveying the scene like a crime reconstruction. This particular man is incidental, collateral for your paranoia, the only thing you'll ever commit to. This man's done nothing to earn the stress test you've laid out in the middle of his evening. He seems sweet and harmless, but so did that other guy with the large, flat face and the firm hands. Wasn't his music taste impeccable, his bedsheets soft, his confidence in slapping you across the face during sex with no warning almost enviable? How random it was, his flying hand, how divorced from the dynamic you thought the two of you had built. You burst out laughing. Oh, bless you, you might as well have said, you think you're a man?

Crucially, this man next to you is not him, and you are not that girl any more, and yet and yet and yet you know how quickly a moment can turn on its axis, how very differently two people can read a moment. What a staggering risk, to trust a strange man with your even stranger body. But you've had all this practice, with these soft-voiced troubadours you've trusted with the fragile mush of your mind.

His thin eyelids flutter for some minutes then settle. He is asleep. You'll make a good anecdote. *Man, let me tell you about this weird girl I hooked up with once.* It's humbling to remember you are group chat garnish to these men, too, flotsam and jetsam on a long stretch of beach. You wonder what his first sexual experience was like. Michael described how his first girlfriend came to his bedroom one night and took off her clothes. As she approached him, Michael covered his eyes with his hands. He was so shy in the frankness of this young girl's desire that he couldn't bear to look at her. I love Michael the most when I think of him this way, his eyes behind his hands, willing the adult world away.

You see my dilemma, don't you? you ask the sleeping man. How could that Michael, my Michael, be just like the rest of them? So cold and calculating, so careless with his hands? Not him. He knew what it was to be scared, to want love, yet be terrified of the adult bodies it came in. Is that why it was young boys he chose? No. He didn't, he couldn't. He understood, he floated above us all. Don't you wish you could float, too? you ask, but he doesn't answer. He is dreaming his private dreams, body calm as a cadaver. I could do absolutely anything to him, you think. It is just a thought, a quick, awful flourish of your mind. You take your hands and lay them over both his eyes.

In an unanticipated twist of irony, being able to sit with how much singers like Michael have meant to me has made the task of holding him to task more feasible. All along, I felt I could not critique and love at the same time. I am slowly arriving at the idea that the former is a necessary aspect of the latter. Crucial, here, is the distinction between love and worship. I used to worship Michael, and worship is a form of annihilation. The godlike figure in that scenario must fulfil the desires of their devotees, which necessarily means denying their humanity. Worship has no nuance or gradation to it, no interest in the multiple dimensions of a person or their betterment. It is inherently dehumanising, all the more so because it believes itself to be love. But it is not. Love sees a person for who they are and wants them to be the best they can be. It is precisely because I love Michael, or at least the idea I have built of him in my head, that I must look the ugliness of what he did square in its unblinking eyes.

VIOLENCE

Everyone remembers being bullied, but hardly anyone recalls, or owns up to, being the bully. We all embellish our most ideal and sympathetic selves. Even when we can admit to behaving poorly, we soothe ourselves by listing all the reasons why. As the saying goes, we measure others by their actions and ourselves by our intentions.

It reminds me of a brilliant scene in the sitcom *30 Rock* where Tina Fey's character Liz Lemon attends her high school reunion. The former queen bees approach her, reminding her how cruel she'd been to them. They recall her as spiky and cold, quick with a dismissive comment or sarcastic barb. She is taken aback, remembering only how lonely and excluded she felt at the time. She is suddenly confronted with a different version of her younger self, not as the woeful underdog but a miserly shrew.

Fey's character flails in the face of this retelling. All her life, she held fast to the story of her young self as uncool. Because of this, she'd convinced herself her little jibes had no weight. After all, how can someone so small, so insignificant, make the people at the top of the totem pole feel bad? This belief is girded by a subtle vanity, a desire to live at the top of a self-determined hierarchy. If you decide to fix yourself in the position of 'loser', make of it a masochistic badge of honour, it becomes its own subversive status. There are strange benefits to this decision. As the perpetual outsider, spikiness becomes a justified and noble response to the indignity of social exclusion.

That old dance routine from school is baked into my body. Hand on hip, kick-ball-change, kick-ball-change, point, pout, shimmy. A repurposed hash of moves I'd seen, envied and stolen. It was going to be the ticket. To where I wasn't certain, but I imagined somewhere shimmering and permanent. The rest of the group, who were nowhere near as dedicated, began to resent my pushiness. Today, I struggle to account for why I was so single-minded. Perhaps I thought I was doing the other girls a favour by including them. Or maybe the truth is simpler and all the more damning for it. It's entirely possible I didn't much think about the other girls' feelings at all.

I used to look back at these memories of girl band cosplay fondly. I replayed the conspiratorial looks we would bat to each other just before the bell rang for break time. Over this, I laid a soundscape of helpless giggles, a scene of our tangled limbs in the playground as we worked out how and when to move. Only recently have certain memories of how I treated them re-emerged, the bullish behaviour I conveniently erased or reframed. In this edit of my nostalgic playback, the lens switches from a wide shot of the group to a close-up on me.

Was I a bully?

No!

I don't think so?

Well.

In a generous assessment, my worst crime was being a little

too humourless, blinded by misplaced ambition. But my recollections are too muddled to rely on. How adept I am at blocking out my worst behaviour, rejigging events so I can live with the most palatable version of myself. How little some of us know, or dare to imagine, how we adversely affect others. We have the advantage of living inside our own heads, constantly feeling and integrating how we feel into who we are. This task leaves little space to consider how what we do and say changes how someone else sees themselves.

As children, we unconsciously conduct social experiments to test the measure of ourselves. Casual cruelty is one of many roles to try on for size. We've all borne witness to its power, how it immediately raises the stakes, places us firmly in the driver's seat of a moment. So much of how we make people feel remains unknown to us. I sometimes wonder if anyone from that playground girl group looks back and remembers me as cruel, whether I hurt any of them without realising. I don't know how ready I am to reckon with the gap between my intentions and my impact. It's a question I don't ask myself often, yet it's one I've wished others had asked of themselves when their thoughtless words or deeds hurt me.

I had my own Liz Lemon moment a couple of years ago. Over drinks, a friend and fellow poet asked if I remembered when we first met. I didn't, as is often the case when I try to recall my first encounters with people who are now dear to me. But as his strong memory would prove, we tend to hold on to the first encounters that feel sharpest. This poet, let's call him Rich, had plucked up the courage to approach me after my performance. I was stood by the bar with another friend and, according to him (look at how I cling to this qualifier!),

I had been brusque, barely engaging with his attempts at conversation before turning my back to him and continuing to chat with my friend.

Sounds innocuous enough, I know. But I hated hearing this. I felt angry at my former self and protective of that Rich. I apologised, which was easy to do considering how much time had passed and that we'd arrived, despite that inauspicious start, at a warm friendship. But the fact remains that in the adrenaline-spiked sweep of the night, I'd been unaware of this new wisp of cachet I had. This is an important illustration of power blindness precisely because it is so small. It is a microcosm of how we measure, or fail to measure, our effect on others.

In this moment, one that I had blithely forgotten and Rich had stored away in his head for over a decade, I was new to the performance poetry world. Though it's a DIY scene with modest rewards, it has its own rickety ladder which we were all climbing. I had a ways to go but I had ascended quickly. I was aware and proud of the buzz I'd accrued but not wholly aware of the kudos that came with it. When considering our status, our mind gathers evidence. I had positive responses from audiences and event hosts. People were even beginning to offer me small fees to perform at poetry nights across the country. What I didn't consider was the weight of what my interactions with others might have. What eighteen-year-old, newly thrown into the world of adults, would even begin to consider they might have some sort of social currency? This is the time we are the most self-critical and self-absorbed, all grievance and no perspective.

Just a few months before the interaction, I had performed

my first ever poem at a sparsely attended open mic in a basement of a Covent Garden café. My hands shook the whole time. Miraculous, really, that I could read the words on the paper. I got through it, just. I felt flighty and inexperienced, in awe of those who seemed to command the room. Equal parts hubris and terror, I was obsessed with performing on any stage that would have me and building myself. This feeling doesn't, as it ought, wane in tandem with growing credentials and stature. In some ways, this is good. Survival instinct prevails and sudden tumbles from grace wait patiently for all of us. But the cost of this failure to integrate one's gradually shifting status is what I unwittingly did to Rich, what countless people have done to me, what happens in proliferate ways every day, right this minute, now and now and now. When you assume you don't have the power to truly hurt people, it makes it more likely that you will.

Considering how much I've contorted and debased myself to get it, I'm hilariously uncomfortable with owning any influence I have. I used to think of power as absolute and fixed, that if I had any, it would announce itself wholesale so I could behave accordingly. Besides, I never want to be the obnoxious person overestimating my importance. But it's much easier to lean on the versions of me that have felt small and weak. That version is given the benefit of the doubt, a healthy concession of sympathy and grace for the bad behaviour that may root from those negative experiences. To know your own power, though, is to stop and think about the dynamics in a room not just from your perspective, but everyone else's.

Like most of us, I struggle to feel anything but disdain for older men who pursue younger women. It represents all that is cowardly about chauvinistic men who want not partners who equal them in experience and agency but pliant, fledgling girls who furnish their egos and laugh at their well-worn jokes. This was the caricature in my head for a long while. But when I tilt things at a different angle, I see it another way. Perhaps the older man who flirts with a woman far too young for him isn't gleefully aware of his ability to manipulate and groom her. Perhaps he is more aware of, or chooses to focus on, his waning virility, the stubborn backslide of his hairline, the fact that the glory days of his youth are firmly behind him. He might look at a young girl, and all the nubile freedoms and opportunities he perceives she has, as the one with the power. Perhaps in that older man is the latent young teenager who never quite mastered how to talk to girls or start relationships. Perhaps he is stuck, still trying to make good on the teenage dream of boy meets girl.

This doesn't make his actions any less immoral or distasteful, but it offers reasoning that opens a conversation interested in more than pointing out the problem. What if we assume that men can do better, and we insist that they do? This requires less scolding or stereotyping (though both are cathartic rituals I reserve the right to indulge in sometimes) and more understanding, the kind that reaches to fix rather than dismiss what I see as a relational impasse. I don't doubt that some men act in at least partial awareness of their powers, fully cognisant of how and why they manipulate the people around them. But I don't believe that is all that's happening. I struggle to accept that pure malevolence accounts for all sordid behaviour. This is an easier story to tell ourselves, one that keeps us in a loop of pre-emptive fear and paranoia. If some men are just inherently predatory, then our only task is to avoid them and punish them when they transgress. But why can't we work with a different paradigm, one that assumes sexual grooming is just as likely to be a maladaptive approach to connection as it is a malicious display of entitlement? It's a daunting hypothesis that's not without its pitfalls, but it offers something that complicit silence or corporal punishment cannot.

Michael's father Joe beat the shit out of him and his brothers. Reasons for beatings ranged from backchat, failing to perfect a routine to his liking or touching their father's belongings without permission. His instruments were classic: a branch off a tree, a belt, sometimes the simple flurry of fists.

Michael recalls being so frightened of his father as a child that he would sometimes vomit at the thought of a pending punishment. In a BBC interview many years later, Joseph said he did not know his presence incited this response in his son. 'But if he did regurgitate, he regurgitated all the way to the bank,' was his chilling response. As far as he's concerned, threat of being hit was a deterrent and motivation, one cog in the engine that made The Jackson 5, and Michael in particular, so brilliant. Would he have been as brilliant if there hadn't been that five-year-old boy inside him, pre-emptively flinching?

There's a slow and uneven reckoning happening in black communities around 'tough love'. It's a difficult conversation to have in mixed company and even harder to have amongst ourselves. To our parents, inevitably, we are traitors. They believed their job was to sacrifice and provide, endure demeaning jobs below their capacities for what seemed the obvious pay-off: educated, successful children, able to dine on the manna of modern living.

How could they have anticipated the other Western mores their children would inherit in a dawning age of self-excavation and trauma mining? Our parents were not modelled with the softness we desperately wanted from them, and the endless demands on them as working parents didn't allow space for them to learn this softness, either. There is fault here, but I'm not sure if there is space for blame. One can know and understand all of this yet have nowhere for the pain and anger to live.

In a speech he delivered in Oxford in 2001, Michael reflected on his past, saying: 'I want to forgive my father because I want a father, and this is the only one that I've got. I want the weight of my past lifted from my shoulders and I want to be free to step into a new relationship with my father, for the rest of my life, unhindered by the goblins of the past.' I am moved and troubled by this measured attempt at compassion. It is painfully true. We only get one set of parents, and it is hard to relinquish them even when they betray us. But Michael's words are haunted by conditionality, a goal that hasn't been met. He does not say he has forgiven his father. He says he wants to. He is struggling towards this place but has not arrived, and perhaps never will. It hurts to imagine that someone who could write so cogently on their own abuse could go on to abuse other children. It is one of many contradictions about Michael I'm learning to sit with. It doesn't make sense. I want it to, but sense cannot be forced from the chaos.

A violent parenting style is usually a hand-me-down. Joe Jackson was also raised by a strict father unafraid to hit his son in order to 'discipline' him. Being hit when you're young is bewildering, not just because of the physical pain but the realisation that your body is at the mercy of forces you cannot control. When I was young, I couldn't work out how other children felt any sense of repercussions without the threat of a beating. I told myself I was grateful for the slipper. Without it, I reasoned, maybe I'd have been insolent and unfocused.

We form a club, us who grew up in fear of that slipper. We ham up stories of being chased around the house with belts, rubber flip flops and wooden spoons. We exaggerate in the retelling, compete to see who got it worst and who can tell it best. The winner is whoever spins a tale of horror into the grandest piece of vaudeville. And it *is* funny, in its own dreadful way. The slapstick of how we were hit, the cartoonish instruments our parents used. We survive it by laughing. We laugh as adults buttressed by the years that have passed. We are not those kids any more. We can fight back by making light of these dark moments, by retelling these moments in ways that give us our agency back. We can fight back by trying to be more gentle and more patient with the children in our care, knowing we will never be perfect but that we have the luxury of knowing better, the option and the will to keep trying.

Learning How to Punch

Uncle E was a big man. Six foot three, with a barrel chest and a big belly. I'd beg him to splay his hand and cup it over the top of my head like a helmet. I delighted in how small I felt under the canopy of his fingers, like a chess piece he could pick up and place on the other end of the room. When he hugged me, his arms would encircle my shoulders and the world would be briefly muffled by the sheer density of his body.

His hugs were gentle. So was the way he pruned the garden hedges with his worn hand shears, pulling at the dried leaves and putting them in my cupped palms. I'd ball up my fingers and crunch them down to yellow confetti. When Auntie and Uncle would sway around the living room to the slow songs they loved, I'd wriggle with impatience. I craved fast songs, how they made my heart hammer and the floor pulse. I'd press my face to the speakers to feel the flesh on my face shake. The inside of my cheek would mash itself against my teeth.

Uncle fancied himself a thwarted boxer. Frank Bruno and Chris Eubank were his idols, men who looked like his friends and brothers. He claimed he used to win scraps with boys twice his size when he was a skinny kid in Bukoto. The living room was his whenever there was a match on TV. I'd keep my nose in a book while he watched, couldn't bear to look up at what was unfolding. The volume would be turned as high as it would go, Uncle leant forward on the sofa with his elbows propped on his knees. In my peripheral vision I could see his fists jab-jabbing at the screen.

Many times, Uncle tried to explain the rules to me, insisting that two men repeatedly thumping each other was not only a sport, but an art. I hated all of it: the braying of the audience in the shadows, the sickly floodlit ring, how their eyes filmed over like fogged glass. Worst of all was the sound of glove meeting flesh, dull and wet.

Do you know how to punch? Uncle asks me this through a mouthful of stew. I'd always found it difficult to eat in his presence. He didn't treat his food like the plants in the garden. He pressed his meat into his matooke with his fingers, sucking on the marrow of chicken bones. He would suck and slurp, work his tongue along the bone. I'd feel viscerally aware of the fact of the animal in his hands, and my hands, too. I'd look down at the glistening chicken drumstick in my hands, think of shins and necks and feet, the channels of blood that once moved from veins to hearts and back again.

The answer to his question was no. I had never thrown a punch or been in a situation that called for it. In the playground, the rough play that happened was always amongst the boys. Girls might shove or kick each other, but we had other, subtler weapons in our arsenal. I looked down at my hands, unable to imagine them with that much power or precision.

I'm going to teach you, he said. And true to his word he moved the blonde wood table that lived in the middle of the living room. First, he showed me the guard position. He began shadow boxing, his fists moving quick as a lizard's tongue. Despite his stocky build, he was suddenly, delightfully agile. He gently wrapped his hands over my pudgy ones and curled my fingers in. *Never put your thumb inside your hands*, he said. I remember this, even now, when walking in the dark through an unfamiliar neighbourhood, my hands readied fists in my pockets.

He quizzed me: *if a man you don't know tries to talk to you, to touch you, what do you do?* I'd answer by leaping into a squat, sucking my breath through my teeth. I fell into the new choreography, jabbing my fists as quickly as I could. Upwards, towards the chin. Down and across, to the crotch. In front of me was an imaginary man, huge like the Hulk, and with the force of my fists I was causing damage, the once insurmountable wall of him crumbling. Uncle lifted me in the air, whooping. *That's my girl, that's my girl*, he said. Without either of us officially deciding it, we began to greet each other this way whenever I'd visit. We'd drop our heads low and raise our fists, aiming shadow punches at each other. I always made sure to have my thumbs curled round the knuckle, my fists just below my chin. It went on like that for years, Uncle and I pretending to knock each other out. Even now, I feel a flush of warmth to think of it. I miss it terribly.

I got into a fight once, by accident. It was at my cousin Clive's house, where he and his four other siblings were forever jostling with each other. Clive was the oldest, happy to wield his superior height and pointy elbows to terrorise the rest of us. He would sneak up behind me, lick his finger and plunge it into my ear. They called it a wet willy, which confused me because I knew willies lived inside boys' underwear. Though it wasn't a slap or kick, the invasion of it was astounding. A thick, oily jab pierced by the edge of his nail, a hidden part of me invaded. As he tried to sneak up behind me on the stairs, reflex kicked in. I grabbed his wrist and twisted. The heel of his hand pushed my head into the wall, my pogo-heart somehow in my throat. My foot swung up, for which part of him I didn't know or plan. I just needed one, swift instance of impact so everything would stop. Something hard under my heel. His mouth open and horror-movie red. *I'm sorry, I'm sorry*, I repeated as he ran down the stairs wailing the sound for mother.

Violence is not an event. It happens all the time. At any given moment, one person is splitting another open, sometimes out of fury but just as often out of boredom. There is blood, shock, then resignation. It is a self-fulfilling pastime, a way in to the things we dare not or do not know how to say. Or perhaps it's one of our clearest articulations, a proto-language we will always come back to when exhausted by the vagaries of decorum.

When *Fight Club* became a cult hit in the nineties, it spoke to what many men felt was a lost birthright. Warfare and combat were once the focal rituals of manhood and what many return to in lieu of alternative rites of passage. Violence, for all its grimness, is a thrilling reminder of corporeal fragility, what is always at stake in our brutal world. On screen, it seduces and compels with its immediacy. Shamefully, I feel it, the involuntary surge of adrenaline in the presence of violence as it's presented on screen. I have developed an appreciation for the auditory thwack of a well-aimed punch, see the dark appeal of how blood glistens under streetlights. Vicariously, the pretence of a better self can fall away as you watch people rip into each other.

But if I imagine pushing my fist into the open sandwich of someone's face, my first instinct is to laugh. It is, on some fundamental level, a ridiculous impulse. The coarse blunder of unchecked feeling, our animal selves laid bare. I still feel like a child in the face of it. I flinch and look back, flinch and look back. I see how insatiable and destructive it is, but I have no idea if there is any human contact without its presence. When Uncle taught me how to punch, he was preparing me for an assumed 'when' and not an 'if'. That scrap with Clive was the only time I've made another human bleed. It wasn't the victorious feeling I assumed would come with winning a fight. Even now, the memory of his dark red mouth makes my chest constrict. But I wouldn't be surprised if it doesn't feature as a prominent memory for him. Clive was the most energetic of us all, turning every game into a competition or a fight. It almost undid him, his constant need to provoke other kids. It would make him the bane of his mother's life. His teachers soon grew weary of his terrorising ways, and by the time we were teenagers he was the name mentioned by all the adults with a shake of the head, a stoic purse of the lips. I wouldn't see Clive again for several years. All I knew of his whereabouts were the occasional pictures I was sent of him kitted out in army uniform, his cheeky grin swiped from his face, replaced with the quietly murderous gaze of a soldier.

From the screen, Michael gives me a salute. The gold epaulettes on his jacket are a sickly gold, with fringing I'd like to run my fingers through. His whole outfit has many eyes, each of which wink at me until I am giddy. He and his dancers march into a V formation, their knees all stopping at the same high point of their hips. The drums puncture each step. Their arms slash through the air with the sound of swords whistling free of their sheaths. This will have been a sound effect playing through the speakers, like the sound of slaps and kicks in films heightened in post-production. But I didn't know that then. Then, I believed it was their bodies making those sounds, butchering the air into submission.

In 1994, Michael paid a huge settlement fee to the family of his first accuser, Jordan Chandler. This would begin a long tumble from a high pedestal, his public perception collapsing and his legacy hanging in the balance. His public image became spikier, more maniacal. He leaned further into the iconography of state violence. For the lead-up to the *HIStory* album, multiple steel and fibreglass statues were erected of him in major European cities. The statue shows him in his familiar military-style regalia, hands balled in defiant fists beside him.

During the same press tour, Michael went to Moscow, where he marched with a platoon of Russian soldiers. I can think of no other pop star who would have the funds, or the gall, to use the tactics of a Soviet-era despot to recoup their cultural legacy. It's the version of Michael I find most alien and bewildering, perhaps because I recognise the ugly flailing of a bruised ego and how it distorts your choices. This is when he began to use his fame as a threat. He refused to be erased from the cultural landscape without a fight.

HIStory's first half is a greatest hits album, its second, a discomfiting rash of songs full of rage, paranoia and maudlin self-pity. With one hand, Michael waves at his long list of hit songs. How, this list implicitly asks, can you shun the maker of such cultural treasures? Then there's the second half, with songs like 'They Don't Care About Us', its percussion the regular thump of marching feet. In it, Michael crassly compares his treatment by the media to rape and the historic persecution of Jews. As listeners, we are asked to offer conflicting things: sympathy for his plight and also unquestioning deference to his icon status. Like a spiralling dictator, Michael made a literal effigy of himself to try and revive his waning importance.

It's an especially American display of dominance, at odds with Michael's calls for world peace. Who else, these displays ask, is worthy of a level of security befitting a nation? But this fascination with and proximity to the military keeps cropping up, becoming more than an incidental trope and curdling into aesthetic pathology. Worst of all, it didn't suit him. He claimed to hate war, yet in the face of existential threat, he relished its gratifying pomp.

I remain naively pacifist, choosing to believe that we wouldn't have wars if we all collectively agreed not to. I know, how adorable of me. Yet I can't deny the seductive power of organised violence, its campy rituals and inherent excess. Much of my engagement with the police and the army has been through its tools. I have worn camouflage print clothes, used handcuffs as erotic toys. All the while, I have been shielded from its concrete horrors. I have never had to face the realities of war or the threat of police brutality. I have never had to engage with the frightening realities that these items were invented for.

The term 'context collapse' keeps circling my head. Coined by professors Erving Goffman and Joshua Meyrowitz, it's an especially common byproduct of our internet age, where an idea can migrate from its niche silo and into the wider popular conscience where its original meaning becomes muddled in a melee of reappropriations. But when the term was first used in 1985, it was to describe this phenomenon in mass media. Whenever Michael used the props of war in his music videos, the overall effect was never gritty or especially menacing. A gun serves as a flippant narrative flourish, no different to a flipped coin or tilted trilby. A long line of soldiers, like background dancers, bolster his status as King of Pop. But, crucially, these soldiers are not actors. They are genuine instruments of war, destruction and death. Yet here they are ornaments to the dying spectre of a pop star's pride. It is context collapse at its worst, the kind that makes a mockery of the horrors from which these symbols grew.

Beyond Punishment

There were things I expected when I walked into the sex offenders' facility. Walls the colour of cheap vanilla ice cream wasn't one of them. Neither was the distinct lack of foreboding I felt as the guard walked me through the labyrinth of corridors leading to the classroom. At the entrance, forms had to be filled in and all possessions put away in a locker. No phones being allowed on the premises and the heavy doors that had to be painstakingly unlocked then locked behind us were the only things distinguishing this place from a standard state school.

I was there to run a poetry workshop. I was one of many facilitators there that day, each of us running workshops on topics including philosophy, tae kwon do and photography. When I was asked initially, I didn't want to do it. I was flabbergasted to even be asked. Me, the angry feminist, write sonnets with sex offenders? I was incensed by the suggestion, which led me to believe I had no choice but to say yes. The guard led me to my workshop room. Inside sat nine men. At a guess, they ranged from their mid-twenties to a white-haired man in a wheelchair who looked to be in his seventies or so. Is it crass to say the sight of them was an anticlimax? Though I'd agreed to spend the next two hours discussing poetic techniques with them, there remained a barbed edge to my expectations. Did I imagine that every man who has sexually forced himself on someone might share some immutable mannerism or physical trait? I believed myself a righteous adversary, but simpler and uglier than that, I was a voyeur, no different to the people who once gathered to watch public hangings of criminals.

I don't know what I expected: bow-backed men lurking in

dark corners of the room, frotting at their thighs with eczema-flecked hands? A cluster of hollow-eyed creeps filing my image away for their sordid masturbatory efforts? I had to chide myself for my own vanity. Just because they were sexual deviants, it didn't mean they were indiscriminate. Still, I'd made sure not to wear anything that even hinted at a body under my clothes. My make-up was minimal, my hair swept up and away in a dark headscarf.

I will say here what I say every time I relay this story to people, even as my trust of this recollection wears thin each time I tell it: they were some of the warmest men I have ever encountered. Even now, I feel a misplaced swell of maternal goodwill for them, sat there with their blue exercise books and expectant faces. My formative memories are so replete with men treating me with indifference and hostility that I had figured this would be some necessary form of exposure therapy. If I could survive this scene and take back further evidence of my theory of the irredeemable rot at the heart of men, then I had won. Instead, here were these soft-spoken and painfully polite men who listened intently as I spoke.

They were shy, as people often are in the vulnerable space of a writing workshop. But they were willing and enthusiastic participants, the kind that make my job easy. I can become a listener and observer, experiencing the workshop alongside everyone at their desks. They listened attentively to each other's writing and offered thoughtful comments on the Simon Armitage poem I'd brought along. It was a poem called 'The Shout'. In it, two boys call out to each other across an ever-increasing distance. The men in the workshop shared stories of growing up as young boys, friends they'd lost, fathers they'd feared but still missed. At the end of the poem, one of the boys grows up and joins the army, ends up 'twenty years dead/with a gunshot hole/in the roof of his mouth'. They all seemed to resonate with the bleakness of this poem, its open-eyed lack of redemption.

At the end of the session, the old man in the wheelchair called me over to thank me. He wanted to know if I'd come back and teach again. I made the noises of someone fearful of making promises to a man who I could only assume had little to look forward to. Opening his large black notepad, he showed me a drawing on a loose piece of paper. It was of me, copied from the brochure detailing all of the festival's activities. It was a good effort, faithfully photorealistic. He'd taken particular care with shading the intricate weave of light and shade in my braids. It would have taken hours for him to draw it, hours of staring at my picture.

I don't know what this man did. I don't know the extent, the severity, to whom or for how long, how old or young his victim(s). My desire to know is not wholly noble, has more to do with a sickly curiosity that shames me. But let's assume there is at least one person who walks this earth with this man's face indelibly marked on the underside of their life. They may have had extensive therapy and gone on to live a fulfilling life despite everything. Or maybe they still wake in the night, mistaking their partner's hand against them in the dark as his. Maybe there is someone sleepwalking through the aisles of a supermarket, wondering when they'll stop feeling numb. For someone, this man may be the catalyst for a perpetual 'after', the person they were before, or could have been, forever out of reach.

That was why, through no direct cause of the moment itself (so gentle, so benign), I recoiled as he touched my hand to say goodbye. It was brief, nothing but a brush. I would never have questioned it in any other context. My mind rushed to thoughts of what else that hand may have done. If punishment is what we seek when we lock men like this away, then I can think of nothing starker: our inability to unsee the worst of what such men can do and have done. No matter how much a man moves through or performs repentance, how does someone truly own the truth of what they've done and trust that most people won't forever shrink away from them?

I don't know this man. Maybe he has a partner, children, maybe even a friend or two who still keeps in contact, who holds a full and compassionate view of him in their minds. Whether or not this is 'deserved' feels like the wrong question. There is someone recalling his hand and all the ways it trespassed. I recall how gentle it was over my own. Not clasped. Laid. That same hand that held a pencil and patiently drew a picture perhaps, almost definitely, touched someone who did not want to be touched. Maybe the vigilantes are right and this makes it a grotesque hand. Perhaps it should be cut off, like a thief's hand would in Iran. But my experience of this man remained. There was a feeling of mutual care in those few seconds when our hands met. He could be my estranged father, my uncle, my tortured husband, my former childhood hero. I place all these things side by side, assuming one will excuse or eliminate the other, relieve my brain of the ugly din that still resonates, years later. He offered to give me the picture to take home. I declined, scared of what it might come to mean to me. The last thing I needed was a talisman of that terrible and beautiful moment haunting my house. As I walked back through the corridors with the guard and back out into a world of clear rights and wrongs, I waited for a clarity that didn't come. I walked into that lair of iniquity hungry for a reckoning. The monster I went to see did not materialise. I was presented, instead, with my own face.

★

I am in the green room of a literature festival, wondering how I can surreptitiously go up for thirds at the food table without attracting attention. Hovering by the bain-marie, I feel a tap on my shoulder. I turn around, mortified. A slight, blonde woman is smiling behind me. She offers her hand, says nice things about the set I've just done. We find seats and get to chatting. She is warm and friendly, soft-spoken, with a measured elegance in her gestures. Something about her is familiar to me, and I ask if we've met before. A rueful smile comes over her face. *Maybe you've seen the talk I did online?* she says. It comes back to me: a viral TED talk with her and her ex-boyfriend Tom. Her rapist. I remember watching with lurid fascination and also relief. Rapists inevitably walk amongst us every day, yet other than the blurry mugshots we occasionally see on the news or a true crime show, they remain faceless and anonymous. I had read and heard so many variations on survivor testimony but not a single one from a perpetrator. The crime sometimes felt mythical, the fearsome figures of rapists both pervasive and impossible to envision. In that talk, a man stood up and owned what few men will. To me, it felt necessary, the beginning of actual culpability.

Up until this point, my chat with Thordis had been light and lively. But as we discussed the fallout from the talk, her face slumped. It was clear the reaction had tired and disappointed her. Understandably, the talk sparked strong reactions, with some expressing outrage that Tom saw fit to not only talk about his crime on stage, but also benefit financially from delivering talks and publishing books on the subject. There were several attempts to de-platform the pair. I read many of the comments under the video and a few excoriating articles deriding the talk. My conviction that the talk had been a good thing began to wane. Clearly, it had caused some survivors further pain and upset. That was enough to dismiss it, surely? But then I would find myself pivoting again, unsatisfied with abandoning what had felt like such a galvanising moment. Did the outrage of some survivors take precedence over others who may have found it useful, liberating or at least worthy of discussion? I didn't think so. I want to hope that we can be robust enough to honour and express our discomfort with something without denying its potential usefulness to others.

A few years before this talk, Thordis and Tom wrote a book together called *South of Forgiveness: A True Story of Rape and Responsibility*. The response was decidedly mixed. One reviewer called Thordis' process a 'dangerous kind of forgiveness'. There is both an accusation of her performing the role of an ideal victim and also an imperfect one who wrestled with feelings of desire for her rapist years after the act. The two had slept together a handful of times some years after the assault, with Thordis initiating rough sex in what she admitted was an oblique act of reclamation and revenge.

The size of the platform and the relative palatability of the speaker, a white, educated woman, are brought up as marks against her. But there is nothing to suggest that this approach can only work for women like her. Certainly, Thordis has the profile of a woman more likely to be listened to and published. But concluding that this makes her approach wholly unrelatable or irrelevant to anyone but a small subset of women feels narrow-minded. Crucially, this was the first time I had ever seen a rapist stand in the light where we can see him, owning his actions and attempting to model some form of forward-facing accountability.

That critique also doesn't take into account that there is precedent for this radical approach to managing sexual assault in minority communities. As you can imagine, a lot of people are loath to involve the police in their affairs. Famously, the police have a poor track record when it comes to the treatment of certain communities. What ways have these people found to address harm outside the justice system?

If you care to look, there's a not insignificant scatter of grassroots organisations working in the middle ground between ignoring or jailing perpetrators. There is the charity Circles (tag line 'No More Victims') that operates across the south-west in the UK. They hold community circles for adults and young people who have committed sexual offences or those considered at high risk of doing so. As you can imagine, people with sex offences on their record often struggle to find work, fulfilling hobbies and social connections. The aim of these circles is to provide a judgement-free space where they can share their feelings and frustrations and access support and encouragement around constructive lifestyle choices. The statistics show that one of the biggest factors in repeat offending is lack of purpose and social cohesion, so this sort of intervention is crucial if we want to lessen sex crimes.

The Storytelling and Organizing Project, or STOP for short, is based in California and was founded on loosely abolitionist principles. They have created an online archive where people can share how their communities responded to instances of harm without resorting to police intervention. With no top-down instruction on how things 'should' be done, the different testimonies vary in their approach. One woman detailed her self-instigated poster campaign to warn people about her abusive ex-partner. Another talks about an incident with a revered drumming instructor invited to teach at the cultural centre where she worked. After he sexually assaulted one of their teachers, a series of difficult exchanges occurred between the instructor and the centre, establishing how he might make meaningful amends for his actions. Not all of the stories have satisfying endings, and not all of them necessarily lead with a sympathetic view of perpetrators. But they all share a desire to imagine a system outside prison bars or complicit silence.

I sympathise with the outrage Tom's presence on stage triggers for some. I'll admit that there's an uncomfortable audacity in the whole spectacle. It easily reads as yet another instance of a man soliciting praise and applause for being 'good' enough to own his awfulness, all the while eliding the repercussions. But I can't be the only one tired of the onus being on survivors to speak on their experiences, often re-traumatising themselves in the process, as if that weren't one half of the equation. Until we apply the same level of forensic care and curiosity to the perpetrators' experience, how do we hope to get to the bottom of why it happens so frequently and how we might change it? No one is suggesting that this work is pleasant or guaranteed to erase sexual assault from the earth. I also don't think everyone has the capacity to hold space for this sort of work. If your rage is the only thing anchoring you into your body, then please honour and keep it. But more of us could consider if we might be able to approach this issue more holistically. Given how prevalent this type of abuse is, and how under-reported, we're in all likelihood encountering perpetrators on a daily basis, are close with at least one. The only difference is you simply don't know it yet, if you ever will. So who are we really angry at, and to what end?

When there's no god to subscribe to other than your fellow human, it's hard to build a robust model of forgiveness. With no divine retribution, no Judgment Day or Final Reckoning, how does forgiveness function beyond the rhetorical? Though it comes with a strong ring of Christian ethos, the appeal to turn the other cheek, is there a way to metabolise this in the hearts of people like me who live without the tether of heaven and hell?

In their provocatively titled book *The Feminist and the Sex Offender*, the writer/activist pair Judith Levine and Erica R. Meiners propose a radical shift in how we deal with people who commit sexual offences. I picked it up desperate for something that absolved me, that assured me I was not a rape apologist for feeling something other than disgust and condemnation. Levine and Meiners argue that if we get rid of the Sex Offenders Register, eschew the medicalisation of perpetrators and work from a place of abolition, our resources can be better spent in the prevention of sex crimes rather than the punishing of them. Their suggestions include delivering better sex education and community-focused forms of rehabilitation. It sounds good, if slightly naive in its utopian vision. It's hard to imagine a world where our schools and justice systems would revert to such a radical metric of efficacy. This way of thinking requires a whole new way of constructing consequences and, crucially, a complete overhaul of what it means to be in relationship to each other. Sadly, I don't think we have world leaders anywhere near forward-thinking enough to instigate this kind of revolution.

Nothing will help you access radical compassion like learning your loved one has committed an awful crime. Michael was my canary in the coal mine, my incentive to understand better. For that I am grateful because I'm not sure I'd have arrived at this place without him. Amidst a painful process of reckoning, one racked with doubt and compunction, I've arrived at a wistful gratitude. It has forced me to ask more of myself and my morals, to free myself of the childish fantasy that evil might be plucked neatly from the world like a scatter of errant weeds. Instead, as I slowly came to terms with the potential truth of the allegations, there was a ripple effect in my social circle.

Every month or so, I'd be confronted with a story about someone I knew, liked and trusted who had drunkenly forced themselves on people, behaved in ways incongruent with the 'good' people I believed them to be. Invariably, these stories are shared in low whispers in pub gardens. We share details from the corners of tipsy mouths, couched in pauses and tiny shakes of the head. None of us quite know what to do with the information or what our allegiances require of us. There is anger and hurt, and underneath that, a silent mourning for fond memories. It is ugly, disruptive information, staining the entire fabric of families and friend groups. A deep sense of sadness and anger for the person who endured the abuse, probably fearing that no one would believe them, that nothing would change. It is hard to not feel implicated, to wonder how you will ever trust your own judgement again.

There's such a disconnect between the forthright articles I read online during the flurry of the #MeToo movement and these fraught, halting conversations I've had between friends about our friends, reconfigured as abusers. The slogans and righteous ire abandon us. The overwhelming feeling is deep, deep tiredness. Do we confront the person at fault and, if so, what do we demand of them? Does such a confrontation ease the pain of the person harmed or does it just appease the unrest of us bystanders? It can't help but feel that in the mere act of hanging out with this person and clinging on to some hope of their basic decency, we've somehow been complicit.

A common instinct is to collude with the denial. It is too much to bear to contemplate the potential truth of such accusations and what they mean for your relationship with the person. The mind wanders further, to if you have somehow aided or abetted in their crimes. This is especially the case for parents of perpetrators, who face considerable blame and scrutiny for their children's conduct. There are very few examples as to how one loves and supports someone while also insisting that they take accountability for their actions. To both acknowledge the transgression and extend your support to the person usually condemns you to pariah status. With not just your pride but your place within your community on the line, it's understandable why many people refuse a version of events where their loved one is at fault.

In order to imagine a system where Michael, and other

people with sexual urges towards children, might have the support they need to deter them from acting on their impulses, we need to understand a bit more about paedophilia. How it actually operates and how we talk about it as a society are wildly different. There are fewer words more evocative than paedophile. Paedophile. Paedo. Nonce. Kiddy fiddler. It used to bring an involuntary shudder up my back just to hear it. The mere mention of it often provokes wild vitriol from otherwise evenly keeled people.

The sexual assault of children ignites an ire in us that few other acts of aggression do, and rightly so. But often, people's attempts to take matters into their own hands are haphazard. Self-proclaimed vigilante gangs have been known to perform extreme acts of vandalism if they believe someone to be what we elegantly call in England 'a nonce'. In 2000, a thirty-year-old woman named Yvette Cloete came home to the property she shared with her brother in the Welsh town of Newport to find the word PAEDO graffitied on her front porch. She found the incident so distressing that she eventually relocated. Yvette was a trainee consultant. A paediatrician, to be exact. These vigilantes didn't know the difference between a child doctor and a child abuser. These are not the sort of people we need at the helm of our justice efforts.

So let's talk seriously about nonces for a moment, because beneath the sensationalist tales we're fed is a complex issue that needs to be understood to be addressed. Some statistics: estimates of how many paedophiles are in the population have varied widely from anything between 0.5 per cent to a massive 5 per cent. This variation gap is so large because the definition of a paedophile isn't clear-cut. The term is used by most to denote a person who has had sexual contact with children, but the medical definition is sometimes more stringent, defining a paedophile as someone with a primary or even exclusive sexual interest in children. The complicated truth is a distinct proportion of child sex abuse is actually opportunistic rather than desire-led. This means that some perpetrators don't have an exclusive attraction to children but will abuse a child if the opportunity arises.

The inclination and the act are two different things, yet we often speak about them interchangeably. This is important because, like all other attractions, the small percentage of the population who do have an innate attraction to children can do little about it beyond taking hormone-suppressing medications to neuter their sex drive. Paedophiles absolutely can and should manage their urges so that children don't come to harm. But the point here is that a person's likelihood of sexually harming another person is separate from their orientation. Paedophilia is the attraction; sex abuse is the act. The two are interlinked but not interchangeable.

It is not inevitable that a paedophile will act on their urges, and there are many cases in which a person abuses a child for reasons of proximity rather than romantic or sexual desire. Just as we shouldn't conflate the queer status of a perpetrator with their abusive behaviour, it's crucial we don't condemn a paedophile for feelings they cannot help. Shaming people only serves to isolate them, making them less inclined to seek the help they need to manage their thoughts and feelings in a healthy way.

Though the thought of such attractions is unsavoury to many of us, it's important to consider how bitterly lonely and tortuous it is to hold such desires. In a society where even naming the urge is treated as tantamount to committing an offence, we can see why people might opt to hide away rather than seek support. But studies show that chronic isolation is far more likely to lead to problematic behaviour such as seeking access to child pornography or contact offences. As convenient as it would be, we cannot simply push these people to the peripheries.

We put a lot of energy into the public pantomime of catching and punishing sex offenders. It's a paternalistic fantasy of revenge and protection that is more about the performed valour of the protector than the children themselves. If the media were really serious about reducing sex offences, they would report on and discuss the factors that make someone more likely to engage in coercive sexual behaviour. The factors are similar to those that might trigger any other antisocial behaviour: stress, loneliness, depression, a lack of purpose, an adverse upbringing. Like so much of our myopic discussion on complicated social issues, we address the symptoms and not the cause. I'm not saying there shouldn't be robust consequences for abuse. What I am saying is that we should put as much, if not more, energy into reducing the mitigating factors that make abuse more likely.

It is also hard to measure the efficacy of preventative measures. You cannot quantify the abuse that might have happened but did not. But it strikes me that this approach is kinder to all of us: perpetrator, survivor and bystander. In this version of the world, all of us retain our humanity. Of course, because this is slow and intricate work that requires deep compassion for people with ugly impulses, it is easier to lead with our punitive urges. This isn't helped by the fact that abusive people are often chronically unrepentant, experts at dodging accountability and empathy for those they've hurt. But excepting those who fit the diagnostic criteria for sociopathy and psychopathy (which comprises a very small number of people), we have to concede that abuse is, at least in part, a social and communal malaise.

Compassion does not mean we have to 'like' these perpetrators, or coddle their delusions as to why their behaviour is justified. Quite the opposite: the compassion I am talking about is humane but bracing. It holds a mirror up to every one of us and asks us all to own our part in the violent, hostile world we inhabit. It asks for all of us to work, especially those who have caused significant hurt to others. I like to hope it's the start of a more exacting and constructive form of accountability, one that doesn't merely ask for the performance of contrition.

Not every person who abuses others will be open to rehabilitation. But we will never really know how many people are amenable to it until we build a culture where this is sincerely and consistently offered. I appreciate that the plight of a repressed paedophile isn't the most compelling site of sympathy. But my fear is that, without this sympathy, we become passive accessories to abuse. This sounds strong, but I believe that one of the many costs of this current era of rampant individualism is that we've stopped seeing how we each contribute to the culture in which we exist.

In all the tiny choices we make, we either corroborate or agitate the status quo. We either assist in a pervasive culture of violence, apathy and isolation or we move towards community, care and collective responsibility. I propose that we are responsible for each other, without exception. That means that if we wish to take pride in the exemplary members of our society, we must also take responsibility for those who break the social contract and ask what we might do to bring them back into the fold. A single person's actions don't happen in isolation. They happen in concert with the world around them, usually through the influence, or conspicuous absence, of others.

From a young age, the allegories we're given are clear about what happens to 'baddies'. They are killed, locked up, spirited away or humiliated into contrition. Occasionally, the villain of a story might have a redemption arc. More recently, children's films are subverting the notion of clear-cut heroes and villains and sometimes doing away with an overt antagonist. We see this in films like *Frozen* and *Encanto*, where the character that incites the most conflict and tension is considered in their fullness. We see the 'why' behind their selfish acts and bear witness to pivotal moments of reflection and remorse. This is very different to the Disney films of old, where evil stepmothers and wicked princes were rendered one-dimensionally cruel and callous, seemingly evil 'just because'. Popular culture seems to be moving towards a more curious lens on bad behaviour, which can only be a good thing.

We have to accept that some of us have led incredibly twisted lives in which inherited morals were at odds with a civilised world. For them, the violence they've inflicted is not terrible but necessary. What do we say to the Josephs, the Michaels, the R. Kellys of this world, who had their cards so thoroughly stacked against them? They have their own reasons, checks and balances for their actions, their own self-image to fiercely protect. We could decide that their violence overrides any good they did, or could have the potential to do. But I think we would rob ourselves of so much in the process. I like to imagine a world where our imaginations can expand to fit those who have not been gifted the love from which remorse and change naturally spring.

It's impossible to know who Michael would have been without the formative abuse he suffered at the hands of his father. Maybe he wouldn't have gone on to hurt children himself. Maybe he wouldn't have become the superstar he did. None of us can comfortably account for these alternative selves and what they would or wouldn't have done. A world without violence is an impossible fantasy, but I live in quiet hope that we might foster a culture where we are not defined by the worst things we have done or had done to us. We would not have to abandon our unruly feelings to achieve this, either. They can come with us because pretending they are not there would catch up with us eventually. But even when we resent extending compassion to those who hurt us, we might just have to do it anyway. Begrudgingly, stoically, consistently. The alternative is the life we are already living, which to me is unlivable.

DEATH

His appearance was like lightning, and his clothes were white as snow. The guards were so afraid of him that they shook and became like dead men. The angel said to the women, 'Do not be afraid, for I know that you are looking for Jesus, who was crucified. He is not here; he has risen, just as he said. Come and see the place where he lay. Then go quickly and tell his disciples: "He has risen from the dead and is going ahead of you into Galilee. There you will see him." Now I have told you.'

—Matthew 28:3-9

Who wants mortality? Everyone wants immortality . . . That is why to escape death I attempt to bind my soul to my work.

—Michael Jackson

A Legend Never Dies

Yusef, the name he goes by off stage, keeps moving his cup of coffee by its too-small handle round and round in the saucer's indentation. It's not clear if he is nervous or agitated. His eyes flick around the no-nonsense café. It's a place of fried breakfasts for a fiver and wipe-clean tablecloths. Around us sit contractors, in hi-vis vests, chewing matter-of-factly on bacon baps and tuna melts.

We exchange painful small talk for the first few minutes. The foam on his cappuccino dissipates into a thin grey scum. 'I don't usually do this,' he says. I assure him there's nothing to worry about as I fiddle with the Dictaphone I bought online five days ago. This makes the procedure feel more professional, somehow, though I could have just recorded our conversation on the phone. The Dictaphone makes me journalistic and not a weirdo, like Yusef.

Yusef, who responded to my DM quickly. Too quickly. Yusef, who at least four times a week travels around the world with his Michael Jackson tribute act, performing tour dates as well as pop-up appearances at hen parties, bar mitzvahs and, once, a child-safeguarding charity fundraiser. When I raised an eyebrow at this, Yusef stared me out, daring me to say something. Fine. You win, Yusef.

I was hoping he might come in his full Michael regalia, but he is dressed casually in loose, faded jeans and a black jumper. In his face I see a chin implant he has to match Michael's own surgical cleft. It looks restless and animated beneath his skin – I imagine it would bend like ear cartilage if I pressed it with my finger.

'I watched some of your videos on YouTube,' I say.

He tilts his head in what I assume is a gesture of humble thanks. He thinks I'm an admirer. In his most-watched video, the phone camera is positioned at an angle and the stage lights stain the scene in a bloodless, crime scene blue. Everything is present: the loose, sequinned jacket, the white socks and black loafers, the processed coils of hair dangling in front of his pale chiselled face. Yusef's skin is actually closer to olive – part of his preparation routine is covering his entire body in a chalk-white, professional-grade body make-up intended for masking tattoos.

As 'Billie Jean''s itchy kick and snare starts up, Yusef's body jerks into the achingly familiar poses: the hat slung onto the bowed head, the swivel, the cocked leg, the index finger and thumb rub together like an anxious bluebottle's legs. He is a committed student of his subject, I'll give him that. The audience happily shouts along as Yusef cups his ear to implore them to sing louder. But the overall impression is one of morbidity – perhaps because Michael has not been dead long enough, or the edges of his legacy are continuing to fray, but Yusef's act feels like an inadvertent swansong for a time and a feeling long gone.

The industry of celebrity impersonation has the rabid pettiness and tender points of pride typical of niche industries little understood or respected by the masses. I'm a reluctant 'spoken word artist', so needless to say I get it. Within the first thirty minutes of talking to Yusef, the stakes of his world gain fullness and an intricate, rough texture of competing principles: tribute acts, he tells me, sit at the top of the hierarchy. They are inherently superior to lookalikes who are, Yusef says in a rare tone of spite, 'sentient cardboard cutouts'. Lookalikes' craft begins and ends with their resemblance to a celebrity. Tribute acts like Yusef dedicate hours to the complete experience of verisimilitude: voice, mannerisms and ever-evolving shifts in the singer's style.

'And don't get me started out on these stinking holograms,'

Yusef says. Any mention I've heard of hologram acts has been peripheral, invariably met with bewilderment by most people I know. But Yusef believes this technology is a genuine threat to his hustle. 'The checkout machines were the start and now the robots coming for all the jobs. But a hologram can never do what we do. They don't have the passion, the heart, the skill. We touch people. We feel what they feel. These holograms are not the real thing.'

Well, neither are you, I think but don't say. His eyes are shiny with fervour. The mood is fraught, as if at any minute he might cry or flip the table. But I understand his fear. I've read articles about AI bots that churn out novels and poems and are getting closer and closer to producing work of feasible artistic merit. It's a disconcerting feeling, watching your calling be reduced to its crass parts, the humbling realisation that plenty of people would be more than satisfied with these empty approximations of art.

He mentions his friend who is a Whitney tribute, how her income tripled in the year following Whitney's death. Did the same happen for you in 2009? I ask. He nods proudly before quickly expressing the conflict he felt, profiting from the death of his hero. 'But I genuinely believe it's what Michael would have wanted, for me to keep his memory going, keep the fans happy.' This sounds like something he has recited to himself many times, a reflexive mantra keeping the rope of self-regard taut. I do not push.

I want to tell him about what I did last night. On a fan forum, a fan under the moniker xxMJsNumber1Angel72xx lamented that Michael would never again record a song. If he were still alive, she wondered, what type of music would he be making now? Others chimed in with their tumbling, erratic theories and fever dreams, detailing which contemporary producers and songwriters they'd want him to collaborate with. Others stated, with the confidence of people with inside information, that though many of Michael's unreleased songs have been posthumously released, there are many, many more, some better than even the greatest hits of his heyday. How did they know this? Where did this confidence come from? It reminded me of the fantasies schoolchildren spin, claiming to be related to famous people, concocting toys and holidays and friends they didn't have. It's frighteningly easy to believe our own lies and half-truths, though. We colour them in so vividly, enjoy how fluidly they fall from our mouths.

I stopped at one post, where a user had used AI software to produce a 'new' Michael Jackson song. I listened to the eerie drag of its synth track, words that had the cadence of English but were largely nonsense sounds. It was Michael sieved through a cough syrup, the excretion of a backfiring time machine. Not only was it a good song, it was deeply unsettling to listen to. I used to hear rumours that if you listened to certain tracks backwards, there were hidden Satanic messages in them. I wasn't convinced by it, but even the sound of the songs distorted and warped, furling back on themselves, was enough to make me feel like I'd conjured some ominous demon out of its lair.

It wasn't dissimilar from the feeling of watching Yusef perform. From what I can tell, people watch tribute acts for one of two reasons. Either they're too broke to see the real thing, or the original star is dead. I can't decide if I find the popularity of tribute acts endearing or ghoulish. There is something endearing about the whole charade, the choice to delight in an imitation.

There's a knowing collusion between performer and audience that can render the charade oddly sincere. But watching Yusef's homage made Michael himself feel less special, precisely because he mimics him so well. Yusef exposed all the composite elements of Michael's every movement and tic. Watching a professional imitator makes the original act seem hollow. What once seemed electric and elusive is exposed as rote and calculated, less than the sum of its parts.

I ask Yusef if he remembers when he first heard a Michael Jackson song. His older brother was a big fan, he says. They both had to share a boombox over which his brother often had dominion. 'When he was in a good mood, I was allowed to listen to music with him, pick the CD. I always, always picked "Thriller".' This was another thing Yusef did. He doubled his adverbs: 'totally, totally', 'never, never', 'always, always'. He'd punctuate the words with two strikes of his right hand. It strikes me as a particularly unique mannerism, the first thing about him that he doesn't seem to have borrowed from his idol.

Like Clive and me, Yusef and his brother would have dance competitions. He remembers getting carpet burns on his knees from attempts at the lean. 'I loved my brother, but I hated him, too, you know? One moment we'd be laughing and messing around together, the next he was shoving my head and telling me I was a fag or whatever. Which I'm definitely, definitely not, by the way.' This was one of the few times he looked me in my eyes. His were indelibly ringed with tattooed eyeliner. They are not the same almond shape that Michael's were, nor are they the right colour: watery and warm like diluted cola rather than startling obsidian. They do, however, have that forlorn look, a gaze that makes a child lovable and an adult unnerving.

So I have found the seed of Yusef's obsession. A brother he could never quite impress. Brilliance born of spite and score-settling. This feels clear and compelling. But that can't be all of it, surely? He holds a sugar sachet by its sides, enjoying the rainstick sound of the sugar moving up and down its paper tube.

'It's like a kid seeing a rainbow for the first time. Just this complete disbelief, like how is that possible? For a long time I thought he was an alien from Saturn. He wasn't like any human I'd seen before. And I was a kid with not a lot going for me then. School was basically torture. I had a couple of friends but they were into Black Sabbath, AC/DC, that kind of thing. They didn't understand why, what the whole Michael thing was about.'

'They teased you?'

'Not exactly.' He furrows his brow, conjuring images, micro shakes of his head discarding shards of unwelcome memory. 'They just didn't get it, they didn't understand.' He flings his arm out, pointing with his hand at the air by our table as if all his naysayers were stood beside us. 'I just hung out by myself mostly, listening to his music. I taught myself every step alone. The mirror in our room was small: it went from here to here.' He frames himself from head to chest with his hands. 'I'd practise this top half, then prop it down against the floor and practise my bottom half. It was years before I got to see what my moves looked like in a full-length mirror. How crazy is that?'

'But how did it become your whole life, your whole job?' I am trying hard to keep my face the right side of inquisitive. A neutral expression is crucial. He may not have the language or self-awareness to name the roots of his own fixation, but it's my job to tease it out. I must give him the impression that I am, to a certain degree, one of his tribe.

'For me it's about spreading the message of Michael.'

I suppress a wince. 'The message of Michael?'

'Yes, Michael was all about love, bringing everyone together. Every creed, every colour, doesn't matter how old or young you are. We all need love and . . . and music, and that's really what it's about. It's not just singing and dancing, you know?'

I'm pretty sure this is the copy on Yusef's website, word for word. I press further. 'But what does that message consist of, exactly? What are the practical applications?'

He shakes his head, motions silently for another cup of coffee from a passing waitress. 'It's about uniting together through the power of music, being gentle and kind and giving, protecting the innocence of children.'

This last sentence hangs awkwardly, strung on a noose of irony. I go to ask him about this, what he thinks of Michael and his relationship to children and whether he believes the allegations. But a sudden speed bump of remorse folds the words back down my throat. I am not long out of that place of disbelief. Beginning to tell myself that perhaps it was true still jolts. Who am I to push him where he's not yet ready to go? Best to change tack.

I rifle through my tote bag for my phone, hoping a text from a friend will be there, tethering me to something comforting and banal. 'So what do you do in your downtime?'

'Not much. Me and Yanna hang out.'

'Who?

'Yanna. She's my lady friend.'

'Oh,' I say, as he launches into their meet-cute story. I am too busy trying to iron the incredulous look out of my face, but he has caught it. Lady friend?

'We like to eat together. She's a fantastic cook. You want to see a picture?'

As he reaches for his phone, something about the practised efficiency of how he selects the picture from his gallery suggests he takes every opportunity to show this woman to anyone who asks. She is not what I expected. She is unambiguously gorgeous. In the picture, they are sat at what looks like a restaurant in some balmy European city. They are both grinning, her with a thick tumble of dark hair, even little pebbles of teeth and big black eyes. Why does it surprise me to see him in love with someone so attractive, so . . . normal-looking? Loneliness was supposed to be the price for being a Yusef, or at best the company of fellow oddballs.

'We go walking sometimes, too. Oh, and we have two pet lizards.'

'Oh! That's cool!' I offer.

'Uh-huh. Billie Jean and Diana.'

His gormless face softens into a little smirk. We both laugh. I am charmed by this brief glimmer of self-awareness. He has found someone who bears witness to him, loves and accepts his strange mannerisms and the crayon rings of black around his eyes. And she is an MJ fan, like him. Good for them, I think. Good for them.

Imitation is supposedly the sincerest form of flattery. But it sometimes reveals a desire to consume and eventually usurp the admired person. I've felt this, in my own forays into copying my favourite stars in how they dress or act. The fantasy of being in their body was so compulsive, so satisfying, that it could only ever bleed into thoughts of what it would be like to not just be like them but *be* them. Imitation followed through to its truest conclusion is a project of replacement, an act of so-called love turned cannibalistic.

Yusef's website is an eyesore, with a ketchup-red background and gold letters hobbled with unreadable curlicues. A cascade of pictures borders both sides, all of differing size and quality. It has, at a stretch, the inadvertent charm of Reddit, but with none of the knowing irony. In his very long biography, he boasts of meetings with multiple members of Michael's family and close business associates. I assume he talks about these meetings on there to signal his legitimacy as not just an impersonator but an integral part of Michael's social circle.

Listening to Yusef exhort about how Michael's mother welcomed him into their home 'like one of her own', I can't help but think about this desperate need for not just proximity to Michael, but also his private sphere. Yusef seems to believe that the authenticity of his act is reliant on a Method approach. Singing and dancing like Michael was entry level, but in visiting his home and successfully blending in with his loved ones, the implication is that he might seamlessly take Michael's place in the family. It's eerily reminiscent of the nineties horror *Single White Female*, all the more so because Michael is now dead and Yusef continues to sing and dance in his place.

'What did the two of you talk about?'

'Oh, everything. He loved nature and animals and art. He was very goofy, too, such a silly sense of humour.' He is away in a world of recollection, a smile so warm that it seems cynical to dismiss Yusef's belief that he and Michael had a genuine friendship. Who am I to say? Maybe they did. As he recalls snippets of conversations they had, I wonder what questions I would have asked Michael if I'd had the same opportunity. Would we have got along? Would Katherine have treated me 'like one of her own'? Why do I feel, suddenly, competitive?

It's disconcerting to think that Michael could not only tolerate the company of people who were so nakedly in awe of him, but that he frequently courted such dynamics. He is praised for his generous relationship with his fans, some of whom had many interactions with him spanning years. In blogs and hastily self-published memoirs, these fans recount these moments fondly. No doubt, all of them believe their bond with Michael to be special. But what kind of friendship can build from such an uneven foundation? When one person is in awe and the other must field this adulation, it's hard to imagine any healthy relating can develop. And now that Michael's gone, people's recollections have taken on a gloss that all our stories of the dead do. We imagine our connections with them as sharper, more profound and singular than they were.

Yusef is, as you'd guess, very angry at the resurgence of stories about Michael's alleged abuse of children. 'Money. That's the problem with the world. People will say anything to get their hands on quick money.' I nod at the truism, though I'm not convinced. He's pulled himself up in his chair. His shoulders are up by his ears. I have done it now, set myself up for war with a diehard fan. There are easier, less exposing ways to seek out money, I say. In the face of Yusef's righteousness, my voice is skimmed of its conviction.

Yusef's spiel unfolds, as flawlessly delivered as an actor's monologue at the emotional peak of a play. It's a thorough patchwork of deflections, admonishments and digressions. Like all good conspiracy theories, there are enough partial truths and logical summations woven through it for an already ambivalent or sympathetic listener to feel convinced. Yusef isn't wrong about money. Americans in particular are comically litigious, forever suing and counter-suing each other. In a world where too many of us are held down by the imperative of money and how we might get more of it, extortion isn't an implausible idea. But in the case of Michael, it feels like a lazy alibi, especially in the face of all the other evidence.

'Also, he was found not guilty of all counts, in a court of law. What more do people want?' he offers for good measure. This is also true. I don't know much about the law, but I do know that it is not as airtight a system as we would want it to be. Despite its wooden courtrooms and stone buildings, its strident language and web of carefully woven clauses, slippages abound, especially when defence lawyers are highly skilled in exploiting the ambiguities in sexual assault cases. Sexual violence is so often invisible in the marks it leaves, happening under the cover of closed doors.

Poking at the sour feeling in my stomach and wondering if it has a name, I rest on one word: pity. I felt desperately sorry for this man and his extreme choices, how strange and pathetic they inevitably must make him to all but a small scattering of similarly preoccupied superfans. He had doomed himself to the life of a doppelgänger, an uncanny apparition.

But then something else came – I was startled and affronted by it. It was (say it) envy. A begrudging respect. Yusef has taken his obsession and run with it, not bothering to tangle himself in the cursive knots of irony or self-defence. He respects his own heart, the nagging thrust of his preoccupations. Is that not the braver and more honest route? Not like me, the supposedly dispassionate observer opposite him, believing myself better because my fixation manifests in a somewhat scholarly way? But it's a fixation nonetheless, no matter how obedient it is on its little leash.

'It's nice to talk to a true fan, someone who understands,' Yusef says as we leave the café. We seem to have swapped moods since the start of the meeting. He is bouncing on the balls of his feet, sprightly and self-possessed. He reaches into his backpack and pulls out a Ziploc bag with what looks like a white handkerchief in it. 'It was his. I brought it for you, as a gift. I thought it would be a good luck charm, as you write your book.' I hold the bag in my hands, flooded with awe and guilt. I try to refuse the gift, embarrassed by his sincerity and my excitement at having something Michael had touched. But Yusef insists I keep it, holding up his hand in a presidential wave before walking away and back to his life of servitude to Michael's legacy, back to his lizards, his loving girlfriend, his unwavering faith in Michael's innocence.

Michael's final magic trick, slipping away just as he promised to dazzle us for the last time, felt like a soft launch, a preparation for life's hardest moral. It was my first time reckoning with the absurdity of death. I was lucky. I got what most do not when someone they love dearly dies – I got to live in a world which, for a brief snatch of time, seemed to hold its breath at the news. Isn't that one of the mourner's many laments, what poet Lisel Mueller called 'the indifference of nature'? For most, this callously efficient world keeps spinning, unheeded by the slow puncture of personal grief. When we come together for the shared ritual and spectacle of mourning for a famous person, we feel what it might be like for the public to rally behind us in our depth of feeling. As terrorist attacks and global pandemics seem to create a sense of togetherness we can scarcely muster at any other moment, the (physical) demise of a loved star is also a potent social glue, albeit brief and unevenly spread.

But here comes the clear-eyed cynic, unburdened by the lowly scourge of celebrity worship. Their scathing tweet usually reads something like: 'I don't get why people rush to cry about a person they never even knew when [insert recent political atrocity] is happening and no one seems to care about that!!' This never strikes me as the sobering reprimand it's intended to be.

All of us preoccupy ourselves with relatively frivolous things in lieu of Big World Issues – not one of us can claim to firmly elide the mini-dramas of our own making in favour of whatever war is happening across the globe. And if we look not at the person but the ritual they permit in their honour, it is rarely just about the person who has died. We all of us carry grief unaddressed and unnamed, all to retain the miserly sceptre of 'dignity'. So, yes, some of us find ourselves unusually disrupted by the death of a beloved pop star. It is not just the star we mourn, but all the other moments of mourning we've denied ourselves.

The shadow of celebrities' influence over how we live is how they influence our deaths, too. When rates of suicide were shown to momentarily spike after the deaths of much loved figures like Marilyn Monroe and Kurt Cobain, research was done into the effects of celebrity suicides and how they are reported. As with their lives, the official and unofficial narrative of these deaths is steeped in the lore of the suffering artist whose gifts ran in tandem with their demons. The method of suicide is treated as an extension of their life as allegory. Journalism has had to reckon with this quandary – the very sensationalism that sustains their business can also create more harm. Now there is a clear precedent in how celebrity suicide is discussed in our media. Methods are not divulged and speculation is kept to a minimum.

Celebrity death is also fertile ground for flights of macabre fantasy – conspiracy theories involving government malfeasance or murder often abound. Cobain's wife Courtney Love has frequently been accused of killing him by his fans. Murky stories swirl around Marilyn's ghost involving rumoured links to bloodthirsty communists in Cuba and the Kennedys. Almost immediately after Michael's death, there were whispers of foul play on the part of his doctor. His physician Conrad Murray had only been working with him for a few weeks when he administered the fatal dose of propofol that killed Michael. Though he was prescribed the drug as a sleeping aid, propofol is primarily given to patients in a clinical setting, often as a pre-surgery general anaesthetic. Murray was eventually convicted of involuntary manslaughter in 2011.

The involuntary manslaughter of fame – aren't we all guilty in this conviction? Don't most of us have a finger on that trigger? Was it not our white-hot hunger for every morsel of information we could have on Princess Diana that spurred the paparazzi into that Parisian tunnel? Is it not in how we revere fame and its hallowed members while also vilifying their efforts to cling to it? Fame kills.

The floor around my workspace is littered with the corpses of dead Michaels. The most recently dead still has the pallor of a live person, but I can see the last of its breath whistling from the body. In writing this book, I have had to kill my hero, the Michael I knew as a child and the Michael I clung to even when all sense and evidence demanded I let go.

We all have our heroes, famous and not, divine or banal, and to relinquish them is a grief that we have no language or ritual for. Often, our heroes die slowly while the person lives on, talking and living exactly as they always have. It is you who has changed, you who must administer the poison to induce their never-ending sleep. But when you kill a hero, their death doesn't mean they disappear. You are left not in peace but with a stubborn ghost. You can befriend it or resent it, but as I've discovered, it remains a permanent resident.

My mother usually went to work early in the morning and was gone by the time I woke up. On the 24th of June 2009, the top of my mother's face skimmed the bottom rung of my bed frame. I could see her forehead and her eyes, her black curly wig. She woke me up so gently. Why my thoughts didn't go to someone in my family, to Uncle or Auntie, I cannot fathom. My mother would not be the first to know if any of my school friends had passed. So my mind made its lightning-quick calculation. All she had to say was his name.

Hindsight is probably doing its revisionist dance when I say this, but the moment before I learnt he was dead, I somehow knew. Perhaps because his death is now an immutable fact, it's hard to imagine I was ever blindsided by it. The night before, I floated on erratic waves of not-quite sleep. My phone buzzed once, twice in the middle of the night, throwing long strokes of light across the walls. No one ever texted me in the middle of the night. Somewhere in my subconscious, I registered that something bad had happened. At least that's how the moment arrives to me now, dripping in portent.

But how could that be true? There'd been no rumours of declining health. There was the shaky prospect of his comeback show at the O2, with its weary title 'This Is It'. The final curtain call, he called it in the London press conference, pumping his arms up and down as the surprisingly paltry crowd cheered. He kept reiterating those words, this is it, this is it, like a weary parent to a greedy toddler. He really means it this time, he insists, his hand splayed in front of his face like a stop sign. His huge sunglasses obscure his eyes, his face skeletal. Watching back, the whole thing seems steeped in doom. But that's hindsight again, indulging me with a sixth sense I didn't have. I think I mainly felt a faint reprisal of my old enthusiasm for Michael. Maybe I might get a chance to see my hero live. The thought gave me an impotent thrill of expectation.

On the day his death was announced, Mum sat and ate breakfast with me as we watched the news. She seldom cried, but that day her eyes were wet with disbelief. I had to remind my body to perform its mechanisms, yell at my feet to move me forwards, at my hand to lift a spoon of cereal to my mouth. Nothing felt real. The TV played an endless reel of Michaels. Wide-nosed, afroed, pint-sized, gloss-permed, Grammy-laden, bleached-out, Messiah-posed, court-shamed, half-starved, hollowed-out – all of them dead, dead, dead while I was somehow meant to put on my uniform and go to school, grow up and older without him there.

At school, where a surprising amount of kids were also feeling the shock of it, I set up solemn vigil. I had rummaged in my drawers for an old T-shirt I'd made when I was twelve. On it, I'd drawn an eighties-era Michael in fabric pen, his faithful corkscrew curl of hair, his huge aviator glasses. Over many washes, the black pen had faded to a pale green. As I struggled into its armholes, I remembered that five years had gone by since I'd last worn it. Puberty had done its voodoo. Michael's face stretched and distorted against my boobs, and the T-shirt's hem stopped before my hips, leaving a slice of stomach exposed. Everything felt out of proportion and hideous. I was very far away from the girl who had drawn that picture. She'd assumed so much about how it would feel to be older. And there I was, closer to adulthood than I'd ever been. I wanted none of it. All I wanted was to shrink back smaller, to curl back to when he was still alive, when I was small enough to believe in things like angels and heaven and eternal life.

All day, the teachers' voices slid past my ears like white noise. But when the end-of-day bell rang, I didn't want to go home. I'd entertained the thought that it wasn't true, that I'd imagined the whole thing. I knew if I went home and turned on the TV, it would confirm what I couldn't bear to believe. I walked slowly home, past the rough-looking park with its rusted swings, the cornershop that sold us bulging paper bags of Pick 'n' Mix for 30p. I forced myself to move in slow motion, dreading my arrival at the house. It didn't matter how long I took. Mum would still be at work. There was no one waiting for me. I stood outside the front door for a long, long time. I remember the cold feeling on my cheeks. They were wet and itchy. I remember sitting down on the dusty ground outside the house with the key in my hand, waiting for his death to become untrue. I am still waiting.

Let The Mourners Come

By the time I was three, Michael had died many times. First, there was Motown Michael: as small, cute and brown as a freshly dropped conker, his father's nose spreading softly across his face. He died in the twilight of his teen years, replaced with a ghoulish doppelgänger: that lovely nose pinched taut, his previously plaintive eyes even softer and sadder, brown skin now the uneven beige of creamy coffee in need of a stir. But this man died, too, and in walked a translucent one, stretched into biker's leather. A lacquered wig tumbles over his face, his chin dented with a cleft borrowed from the faded MGM era. Though heavily ringed in kohl, the eyes remain faithful, the only part that reprises with every ascension. Michael jangles with every step, a BDSM tangle of buckles and straps, a Houdini trick in reverse. He keeps dying and coming back to life, usurping Jesus in his countless reprises.

I remember, or think I remember, asking my mother about it. The skin. Or was it Auntie E who fielded all my questions? Maybe I asked each of them at different times, looking for fragments that might add up to a coherent whole. I never got a straight explanation for Michael's changing hues. They would shuffle their deck of answers and draw one at random, trying to convince me, and themselves, that they'd hit upon something that made sense. Their evasive answers were annoying at the time, but now I understand. It's an impossible lesson to impart to a child: even a titan like Michael could not survive the fact of his blackness.

There was talk of a skin condition. I repeated it to myself, enjoying the frog leap of the syllables: vi-ti-li-go. My mother mentioned an act unknown to me before I heard it then: bleaching. Bleach? Surely not! My only reference was all the bottles of cleaning products kept in the cupboard under the sink. Their labels said things like 'DO NOT DRINK' and 'If contact is made with eyes seek medical attention immediately'. I unscrewed the cap of one and sniffed. It had a waft you could feel at the back of your eyes. It smelt like hospital corridors. How did it work, I wondered? An absurd image visited my mind of a person on their back holding a bottle above them, a stream of neon bleach pouring on to them like an inverted baptism. Did it not stink? Did the skin not sizzle, break, blister? I asked follow-up questions. How did bleaching work? Was it a one-time thing, or something you had to do over and over? Why, why, why would he do that?

As a nineties baby, I witnessed Michael's transformation in reverse like a slideshow of photo negatives. I never shared a planet with the black Michael. He was already a throwback to a foregone era by the time I was born. With all the album artwork laid side by side in order of release, I could see the story of his transformation in increments. *Off The Wall*, *Thriller*, *Bad*, *Dangerous*. Even the titles themselves pointed to how bonkers it was. It occurred to me that my mother would have watched this unfold in real time. As the late seventies tipped into the eighties, what did people think of Michael's slowly paling face? How did it feel to witness the slow death of the first black lodestar? Michael was the first black superstar to seemingly transcend his skin, not just in how his music was received but in how he was seen and spoken about. All the markers used to categorise the rest of us were laughably ineffectual when it came to him. But as he gradually stripped himself of his colour, the topic of race anxiety, his own and that of an entire generation of African Americans, was brought to the surface.

Still. I've grown somewhat protective of all these iterations of his face. Even at his ugliest and most bizarre, he is beautiful to me. Every contortion and crater, the shrinking nose and the audacious thatch of those lace front wigs . . . I know and accept it all. Loving Michael was like loving anyone. It was living with the constant, maddening fact of change and decay.

> *Michael Jackson's music isn't a meal. It's more elemental than that. It's the salt, pepper, olive oil and butter. His music is how you start. And the music made from that – that music is everywhere, too. Where would the cancellation begin?*
>
> —Wesley Morris

Long after his death, Michael keeps coming back to life. I am comforted by the fact that culture at large seems as loath to let him go as I do. Everywhere I look, he is referenced, honoured, parodied and emulated. Our culture is forever haunted and indebted. The rapper Offset rocks a sequinned glove and matching military jacket on the red carpet. A dancer in an Ice Spice video twerks for the camera, the word BAD graffitied on her cropped sweatshirt. There he is in Daniel Bedingfield's yelps and Beyoncé's Super Bowl costume and Usher's poses and Christine and the Queens' footwork. A clip goes viral of a kids' dance team winning a national competition. They are dressed in white suits and trilbies. As they lean, it reads like a bow to Michael who shows up again, a day later, in a clip of Jennifer Garner shuffling through the 'Thriller' choreography in rom-com classic *13 Going on 30.* It is shared on my timelines thousands of times, comments reminiscing on how people did the dance in their school days and how their kids also know it by heart. Here we are, Michael's tireless exhumers.

And all the while, Michael's estate continues to generate millions every year. In 2021, its value was estimated at $115 million. He is, by a country mile, the highest-earning deceased celebrity, worth far more dead and buried than he was in the last decade of his life. No longer is he swallowing up his own revenue with the pesky costs of his spiralling debt and lavish lifestyle. The celebrity estate lawyer is a wily scavenger, descending on the treasure chest of a star's assets and mining it for everything it's worth.

Songs casually thrown onto the studio cutting floor are repackaged as 'exclusive bonus tracks'. The ephemera of letters and diaries are pored over and sometimes published. Then there are opportunistic writers like myself, using celebrities as anguished allegories for our myriad neuroses. The dead celebrity doesn't get to rest in peace, often working harder in the afterlife than they did as a living being. Their memory is evoked, earnestly and cynically, to boost ratings, clout and revenue.

Out come the greatest hit complications, the commemorative T-shirts, the limited-edition vinyl and reissued posters. Footage of old interviews takes on a prophetic sadness. Suddenly, every banal, derivative thing they said is laden with significance. The imminence of their death is written across every blink or grimace. And now, in the restless kaleidoscope of social media timelines, our collective grief is bolstered by looped clips of the star in their prime. And they're always young and in their prime when we commemorate them, aren't they? We memorialise the convenient parts of them, frozen in youth and beauty. The parts of them and their story that we do not like, we bypass.

A famous person belongs only partially to themselves. A dead famous person does not belong to themselves at all. We, the insatiable public, are finally free to project all our fantasies onto our heroes. What a relief that they cannot talk back, inconvenience us with their pesky humanity.

It must be weird for the families. Their loved one is a piece of cultural real estate first and a human second. Imagine walking down the street and hearing that person's song floating from a café's open window, looking up to see their face smiling down from a giant billboard for a cash-grab musical. Grief is strange enough without this cannibalising. But then again, it might be a bittersweet comfort to watch the world honour the mark that person made on the world. It might feel as if your love for them is validated everywhere, the world's reluctance to let them go mirroring your own.

Increasingly, we mourn alone or in small pods of close family and friends, estranged from the ancient rituals that once crystallised and celebrated death as a natural part of life's cycle. In the sweep of modern, agnostic life, we live in muted fear of death and only confront it when we are forced to. Otherwise, we talk of it in strained whispers or not at all. We drift away from people's grief like a fart in a lift; no one wants to be the source of the stink.

We take for granted that people will recoil from our pain, throw their well-worn platitudes in our laps and back away. But when a famous person dies, we see how strong our desire is to lament our losses together. I find myself moved by how briefly unified we can become in these moments. A sceptic would say that the breathless spectacle of grief we enact for dead celebrities is the natural end point of our parasocial culture, and they'd be right to an extent. But I still wish to defend this ritual of ours despite its seeming vacuity. I think it's normal to mourn the absence of people whose art has shaped our lives. Just like our parents, friends and partners, they have accompanied us in the task of becoming ourselves. For some of us, these figures may have felt more consistent in their presence than the people we actually know. Even so, it can be a jarring grief to experience alone, precisely because we don't feel entitled to this assumed grief for a stranger. We want to know that others feel the same. It is right that we reach for each other, right in the moment when we feel most marooned and foolish in our loss. If my Michael obsession has taught me anything, it's that we can be profoundly shaped by a person we've never met, even if that person remains a face on a screen or a voice through a speaker.

To those who reasonably question the validity of my loss, I confess to its flimsiness. It's hard to say what it is I am mourning, if not the flesh-and-blood man. Perhaps that was what confounded me: the betrayal I felt in the face of his mortality. If you present yourself as godlike, you have a duty, surely, to defy earthly capitulations like death? I thought he would live forever, not figuratively or 'in our hearts', but literally. Along with what he did to those children, this is another fact that still bounces off my brain, refusing to take hold.

* * *

There can also be another side to performative grief. A cathartic, competitive edge. In the days after his death, footage of Michael fans outside various gathering places was televised on the news. I remember a crowd of fans meeting at the flagship HMV store in London. They were all dressed in their white gloves and black hats, blasting his songs from boomboxes. One girl threw her hands up to the sky and let out a long wail of despair. It was thrilling, this unzipping of British stoicism.

It was the opposite of how grief operated in my family. No one ever spoke of it. I surmised that death was a tragic thing that happened over there somewhere, a plot point in movies to force tears from the audience. It didn't happen here, to me, with us. But it turned out that people in our family were dying all the time. Sisters, brothers, uncles, aunts and parents back in Uganda. These were the strangers who lived in my mother's photo albums. I would flick through them with the distant fascination I had for history books. Many of the pictures were from the sixties and seventies, tea-stained in sepia. My brain assumed these faces belonged to a hazy past.

Any talk of feelings happened in brief, accidental flashes, like loose change falling out of a pocket. But Uncle's grief when his mother passed defied translation or catharsis. Many years would go by, and he would not talk about it. No one in my family expressed the latent grief of the half-lives they lived in a country that remained ambivalent to them and them to it. Family members became nostalgic ornaments, old bruises. Distance surely became its own form of death, a deferral of more fatal forms of loss.

When Mum would chivvy me into speaking to relatives from Uganda on the phone, I used to hate the lag between a question and its answer. Often, the response would come once you had already started another sentence. The conversation devolved into a series of missed connections and reversals, repetition and negation. That painful pause, waiting for the person on the other end to speak, who was also doing the same. All potential for connection dies in this waiting space.

We are not supposed to grieve like this. In New Orleans, they dance through the streets with coffins on their shoulders. Tibetan Buddhists conduct 'sky burials', laying their dead out in the elements to be eaten by birds. The Tinguian people dress their dead elaborately and display them in their front rooms for loved ones to come and pay their respects. Sometimes, a lit cigarette might be propped inside the body's mouth for good measure, perhaps the only time smoking can be considered a full pleasure with no consequences.

But our modern aversion to confronting, and accepting, death means we hide the bodies of our loved ones from sight. We don our black suits and dresses, mumble through our hymns and read the elegiac poems we find on the internet. We tuck the unruly parts of grief away, where no one can see them. All of this in service to dignity. What a heavy, scolding word is dignity. It means both 'worthy of honour and respect' and 'a serious, composed manner'. Does the latter necessitate the former? Who decided this? And what parts of our humanity do we lose in service to this?

My mother says the first time I saw the 'Thriller' video, I hid my face in the sofa cushions and missed all the cool dancing parts, refused to sleep in my own bed. On further viewings, I cowered at how they moved their bodies, oozing out of their graves like pus from spots. And their faces! The molten droop of their skin was horrific, as were the spare, sweetcorn-coloured teeth hanging from their gums.

Now that I know every beat and frame like an old friend, I see the fun in it. I've grown fond of the zombies and dabble with different allegiances. Currently, my favourite is the one who opens his mouth in a yawn, a glossy black ooze dripping like sickened honey from his mouth. Poor things. They cannot help how they are or what their bodies have become. Imagine you were met with screams of disgust whenever you dared to poke your head out for a little air and a boogie with your other undead friends. Maybe we should consider them worthy of admiration. It is quite the feat, surviving death.

Mourning Memory

Memory, like liberty, is a fragile thing.

—Elizabeth Loftus

On the right of my forehead, I have a scar the size of a Tic Tac. The skin is shiny and ridged like a worm's. It's the best kind of scar to have. It offers a point of interest on my face without being wildly distracting. I got it when I was five. According to my mother, I tried to stab my own head open with a kitchen knife. According to Auntie, I was playing with the knife and tripped. It happened at her house, the two of them chatting away in the living room while I pottered about in the kitchen, looking for the objects that carried the most intrigue and consequence. They both agree I managed to come into the living room with the knife in my hand with neither of them noticing. Only when I yelled out did they turn around and notice what my toy of choice was. I suppose this is a running theme for me, a restless need to poke and prod in shut-away places, to test a sharp edge's bluff. It was the first and last time I'd play with knives, but it is not the knife that troubles me about this story.

My memory of this moment is both vivid and context dependent. I recall events differently depending on whose version is foremost in my mind. Sometimes I remember, or feel I remember, pushing the tip of the knife to my head. Other times, I remember my body lurching forward involuntarily, so much so my body will make a tiny lean forwards in the remembering. Both feel true, though of course they can't be.

My mother and Auntie have both told the story so many times, alone and together, with their own variations and differing details, that I've learnt to think of it as a movie with different edits. I'll never know for sure if it was an accident or an inexplicable burst of fatalist daring. They both recall the taxi to the hospital in the same way, though. I do, too. I like to think of being sandwiched between them in the backseat, both their faces soft with worry, a crumpled flower of tissue pressed against my leaking head.

Elizabeth Loftus would probably say my memory has been manipulated. She believes this happens more often than we think, with far-reaching consequences. Loftus is a psychologist who studies the phenomenon of memory, and in particular memories of traumatic events. Her controversial claim is that the truth of repressed memories is not unquestionable. Her life's work has been studying if and how people have false memories planted into their minds. She has cited the use of language manipulation and the hope for financial reward as factors that encourage the development of false memories.

In one of her studies, participants were asked to watch some brief footage of minor car accidents. Afterwards, they were asked to estimate the speed of the vehicles involved. People who were asked 'How fast were the cars going when they *smashed* into each other?' gave higher estimates than those asked 'How fast were the cars going when they *hit* each other?'. As well as dedicating her research to this burgeoning department of neuroscience and delivering a popular TED talk on this subject, Loftus was actively involved in the court cases of several high-profile celebrities, including Harvey Weinstein, Ghislaine Maxwell and Michael Jackson in 2005.

Wade Robson was a star witness in Michael's second court case. His staunch denial of any abuse played a not-insignificant part in Michael's eventual acquittal. Since the first allegations in the early nineties, Wade went on record multiple times denying any inappropriate behaviour from Michael. As you can imagine, detractors have questioned the truth of his most recent claims. Why did he lie as a child, and then as a young adult? Why was he saying all of this now? Unlike other adult survivors whose suppressed memories come to the surface years after the fact, it doesn't seem that Robson had blocked out what transpired between him and Michael. Rather, his infatuation with Michael meant he didn't compute Michael's behaviour as abuse until much later.

Rare is the abuse story that cannot be pulled apart for holes and inconsistencies, if that's what you're intent on finding. Sexual abuse cases are notoriously thorny for this reason. Their verdicts are predicated on proving acts often committed in private and hinge on the often scattered testimony of traumatised survivors. I personally find Robson's testimony moving and believable, but what's especially noteworthy to me is how our relationship to what we remember can morph. With distance and a different lens, what once seemed benign is reimagined as sinister, even if it didn't feel that way at the time. This is what I find most unseating: that the most pertinent part of our memories, how we felt at a given moment, can change and warp with retrospect. For those whose abuse didn't register as unambiguously violent or coercive, it makes sense that the victim label is disarming to adopt. Self-blame is a common anguish amongst survivors of child sex abuse who recall 'enjoying' or even craving the attention of the abuser.

Loftus maintains that therapists have been known to convince their clients that they've experienced abuse that didn't actually occur. What reasons does anyone have to do such a thing? Pointing to watershed moments like the sexual abuse scandals in the Catholic Church, she suggests that therapists were pressured to generate testimony in support of a culture newly obsessed with detecting historical sexual abuse. Those ideas won't sit comfortably for a lot of us, and for good reason. It's been hard work to create shifts in social attitudes such that more of us lead with compassionate belief when people make claims of abuse and exploitation.

But, to some degree, Loftus is right. Our memories are not the solid artefacts we might hope or assume. If you've ever swapped notes with someone over a shared experience, you'll know that memories can be partial and selective and also change over time. It could even be argued that memory can be a vanity project, a process of shaping, smoothing and erasing to aid the story we wish to tell about ourselves.

Loftus's research has troubling implications for how we process the world, creating a whole new layer of scepticism that can quickly become debilitating. If we can't trust our recollections, then what can we trust? I've not been quite the same since engaging with her ideas, especially as a writer who pulls from memory in my work. It has made my grammar more slippery, my statements more likely to shift and pucker like tectonic plates. It's a death of certainty.

Scientists often frame themselves as chaperones to our untamed emotions. They come with their studies and statistics to chastise us for leading only with our emotions and instincts. But even Loftus isn't immune to having her personal allegiances colour what she will and won't stand by. Though she's used her research to consult on cases for notorious serial killers including Ted Bundy, she drew the line at working on the case of John Demjanjuk who operated gas chambers in a Polish concentration camp during World War II. Being Jewish, Loftus declined this work so as not to upset her family and friends. None of us are wholly rational or impartial beings, though our lauding of our scientific and legal systems give us the false impression that we are.

What do we trust in the face of this? On what do we build a robust notion of truth, of justice, the intrinsic shape of lived experience? We can't go back to when people's claims of abuse were so easily dismissed and minimised. But how do we reconcile this with the brain's capacity to distort events and, in turn, our capacity to distort that fact to potentially nefarious ends? Here is the perfect theory for anyone committed to sowing seeds of uncertainty or holding on to a version of events that absolves them of any responsibility for their actions. Considering that how and what we remember informs who we are and will decide to be, it's important that we take our memories seriously, that we remain curious about how they can morph and set and morph again.

HOME

All The Houses I've Ever Haunted

I am stood outside a squat house on a run-down suburban street in the former industrial city of Gary in Indiana. It has a mixed facade of white wooden panels and grey sandstone and a modest front garden. It is utterly unremarkable, aside from the fact that the biggest pop star in the world grew up here.

This trip has cost me four hundred and twenty-five pounds and three thousand, nine hundred and thirty-one miles. The roof of my mouth still tastes earthy from the thick mushroom sauce my airport meal was drowned in. The back of my neck is tight. I cross the road and approach the front gate, circle the perimeter of the house like a furtive burglar.

The house has two bedrooms, in which Katherine, Joseph, Michael and his eight siblings slept. We are not allowed inside, so I have to imagine what the rooms are like: an obstacle course of bunk beds, perhaps, a single bed in which three skinny kids slept top to toe. The front lawn is lurid green and trim, the asphalt on the pavement is cracked with fissures.

It's a cold Tuesday in early March, and I am one of a paltry handful of visitors. An Asian couple walk gingerly up the path of the house hand in hand, whispering nervously to each other. To my left, a white man takes pictures of a teenage boy, who stands and grins outside the house, double thumbs up, his bright red braces gleaming. On his white T-shirt, a silhouette of Michael frozen on its toes.

After watching their awkward attempts at getting a selfie, I offer to take a picture of them together. The man clasps the boy's shoulders, as if he were trying to plant him into the ground. Their faces break into matching, gummy smiles. I so wish to be them, to be part of their uncomplicated joy. It's the same feeling I get when walking down residential streets at night, pining to live the imagined scenes of harmony behind drawn curtains. The father calls out, greets me in a Southern drawl. *MJ fan, I assume?*

His voice is the small chink of a curtain parted, a face peeking out and looking back. I nod, then quickly turn away, my throat hijacked by a sob. I want to accept this invitation, enjoy a brief moment of communal worship. But as I'm offered a chance to step back into my obsession, I resist. Like we want all homes to be, it is safe, familiar, comforting. I've returned to it over and over, know its contours as well as the walls of my childhood bedroom. But I have not come to resurrect the Michael who once lived in my head. Neither have I come to reinhabit the mind of the young girl with her MJ CDs spread out in front of her. I am here to lay my dying faith to rest. In coming to this house, I am confronted with the physical fact of bricks, roof slate, the needed brutality of facts. I hope this pilgrimage will force Michael's demotion from demigod to human. If my mind can finally accept him as real, then maybe he can be fallible.

If you didn't come here specifically to see it, you could easily walk right past the Jacksons' family home none the wiser to its significance. In that way, it's a ripe allegory for most of our origin stories, which often say more about our retrospective demands on the past than the fact of what actually happened. We look to our beginnings, not for some historical anchor but a coherent, convenient tale of who we've become.

The only marker showing who lived here is a black commemorative plaque on the ground. Under his name, birth and death dates, there is a caption: *You Gave Us A Lifetime Of Love.* I crouch down and run my fingers over it. I immediately feel silly at this self-conscious gesture, the sort of thing an overzealous actor might do. I look to either side of me. The couple are gone, as are the father and son. The only sound is the wind pestering the branches on a nearby sycamore tree.

The urge to pee has ramped up, impeding my ability to walk straight. Legs clamped, I mince to the side of the house, yanking my jeans down and sighing into a feral crouch. The dead grass tickles a shiver out of me. My ears alert for the sound of voices, I unclench my pelvic muscles. My trickle makes its hurried rivulet through the soil. I tell myself it's a libation of sorts. Then I laugh and laugh and laugh. All pretensions I had of restraint or decorum disappear with that steaming jet of piss. It is hot and energy-drink yellow, shameful, miraculous, mine.

Depressing Surroundings! is the headline of one Tripadvisor review I read on the bus back to Gary's town centre. *If I knew the journey would leave me depressed after seeing the ghost town, I would not have gone. You can skip it unless you deem yourself a diehard MJ fan or just want to see poverty all around*. They gave the experience two stars and attached an image of one of the neighbouring houses, its windows shuttered, the front lawn patchy and jaundiced. It's the defeated look of a house left uninhabited for decades. I look out of the window and watch many other houses like the picture move past me. Broken windows, wooden shutters peeled and splitting. The few people on the streets walk alone or in dazed pairs, their clothes a universal palette of black and grey, their eyes fixed to the ground.

The former house of the King of Pop sits immaculate yet empty. Its neat facade is well-kept; someone must be paid to mow the lawn and sweep the yard. The panels outside boast fresh paint; an eerie statue of two children holding hands on the front lawn is polished to a dull shine. If the house became an official tourist attraction with a visiting fee and a gift shop, at least locals might benefit financially. As it stands, Michael's family home has become the worst of both worlds: a potential spectacle but actual disappointment, a charmless ghost house with no dividends for those forced to live in its orbit.

It's true: looking at Michael's childhood home is depressing. It is depressing because so many families lived like this then and live like that now. Even when compared to its rougher counterparts, it is far too small a home for an eleven-person family. Michael's family were unambiguously poor, as are many families in Gary today. The Tripadvisor comments section is replete with visitors affronted by this ugly reality.

Maybe they would prefer a replica of this home positioned in New York or LA. What we want is the narrative swell of poverty's aesthetic divorced from its bleak realities. It would instead be a Disneyfication of poverty, offering its emotive rush and none of its discomfort. It's an insidious voyeurism which demands catharsis without the fear our wallets might be stolen or our consciences pricked.

Michael's hometown was built around the emergence of steel mills and the plentiful work and money they generated. Since the steady decimation of this industry, Gary has slid into a bleak limbo. Thirty-six per cent of the general population live in poverty and eighty-four per cent of its population is black. But in the sixties, Gary was caught in a manufacturing fever and the gradual emergence of a middle class. It was a time when a man might live by the godless gospel of the American Dream and make something of himself. A man like Michael's father, Joseph Jackson.

Imagine Joseph, stood in the bright-eyed myopia of New America. He was in a band in his youth. Of course he was. They were a perfectly adequate ensemble, playing the kind of music that furnishes the far corners of bars on any given weekday – covers and a few self-penned songs. The Falcons, they were called, a blues outfit that met for rehearsals after long days at hard, physically ruinous jobs, each member plagued with their own sense of being hard done by playing music that both soothed and aggravated. Like most bands, they did not amount to much beyond the local circuit. Luck, talent or patience didn't show up in enough abundance.

Now imagine Joseph watching his young son Tito play guitar. Picture his rage that his son went behind his back after being expressly told not to touch his father's precious instrument. This guitar is precious to Joseph, a museum piece from some version of a life that could have played out differently given a little more time or courage, a few less kids. Yet there it is: a young man with half your face, besting you on your own instrument. How proud Joseph must have been – and how betrayed. A decision was made, a swift transference. If success couldn't be his, it would be his children's. He would live on in the proximity of their greatness. In fact, they would be in debt to him as long as they lived. He would forever frame himself as the seed from which they grew, the standard that kept them striving.

The trope of the pushy parent is well-worn. They were born too soon or too late, victims of how and when they were born. Saddled with family life and its self-negation, parents everywhere inflate their children with one legacy: the reconciliation of thwarted dreams. Behind every child pageant star, piano savant and young Olympic gymnast, you are sure to see them lurking, eyes narrowed and watching. They are coach and mentor, cheerleader and slave driver, the voice of the inner monologue a child star will spend the rest of their life running from.

Love Thy Neighbour

Next door, I hear my neighbour yelling at her kids. Through the different pitches of voice that bleed into my flat I guess there are three of them. Every day without fail, the mother's voice leaks into my living room around eleven a.m. She shouts 'sit down' and 'shut up' and 'shut the fuck up', in different configurations and at varying levels of volume. My chest clutches. Multiple times, I have pondered calling the police. What if these children are in danger? But danger is hard to diagnose through a wall. Motherhood is stressful. Common is the child whose life was worsened by state intervention. So I do what we increasingly do in this day and age. I put my headphones in. I mind my business. I fleetingly dream of a home where I don't have to reckon with the endless dilemma of other people's lives.

In these moments, I'm pummelled with the urge to watch celebrity home tours on YouTube. I will sit propped up on my bed with the broken slat that whinnies as I adjust my weight. I probably eat something cheap and salty straight from the packet. Hours will go by as I judge, covet and mourn. 'That wallpaper's a little gauche,' I think, as a rock star's tattooed arm sweeps across the lavish yawn of his living space. Each room unfurls into the next, every outdoor wall a window. A smug churn of natural light falls across a Ming vase, an artfully distressed chaise longue, a counter top that's never known crumbs.

This received fantasy of the ideal home assumes perfection and isolation, separating oneself from the noise and stink of your fellow humans. Luxury homes are set in acres of land, flanked by sombre iron gates. Their seclusion from other homes protects them from the gaze of others, a signal of superiority, an omission of guilt. The rich and famous, for space, safety and status, opt to live tucked away from where most people live.

This is the reward and the punishment of success, to be placed above and away from others. The very urge to pursue fame is rooted in a stubborn belief that one is uniquely talented, deserving and special. Achieving fame affirms this belief, bringing with it the persistent need to physically separate from everyone else.

Most of us do not live this way. We live stacked like cans on a supermarket shelf. Some of us itch against this closeness, buy lottery tickets in hope of multi-floored homes fortressed by high gates. We begrudge each other's loud music and bratty kids, wince at the babble of TV seeping through the walls. There are fewer casual chats over fences. We are tired and overworked, fatally incurious about each other. At best, we pass on each other's missed parcels with little more than a grimace of acknowledgement. This not only precludes us from the love and connection we might feel, but the necessary caretaking and protection that an integrated neighbourhood provides. I fear that if the worst happened to me or the family next door, neither of us would know until it's too late. Worst of all, we'd have no rapport built on which to care.

Is this miserly schema of existence all we can expect? We throw the word 'community' around, but it feels less like a way of being and more a rhetorical garnish. Google Images offers me clusters of smiling white people in quaint villages, landscapes braceleted with thatched roofs and rolling hills. A jingoist's fever dream of pastoral Britain is the original and only bastion of community, this image search insists. In this land of doffed caps and borrowed cups of sugar, everyone knows each other's names and no one locks their front doors. These weren't times free of horrors, but there was at least a sense of shared consequence, lives braided in and out of one another.

Sadly, abusers can operate unimpeded in almost all circumstances. Sometimes it's the distance and indifference of their immediate circle that protects them, other times the wilful ignorance of a tight-knit community. It's my belief that there is no hope for true care and accountability in the former, who cannot bear the repercussions of a meaningful reckoning. A reckoning, I must stress, doesn't necessarily take the shape of rubbernecking, of reporting and shunning and social exile.

These acts are inherently othering and hostile, tools of the state that make us feel further apart from and suspicious of each other. Ultimately, it's the tight-knit community that has a better chance, and greater incentive, to create a world where I might knock on a door and ask after the family inside as if they were my own.

Every Tuesday, I come to an old church hall and push open the heavy door with my shoulder. This is where a steadily rotating warehouse of donated food is kept. In three hours, we weigh, date and sort the items before they're delivered to various food banks across the city. In the corner, an old radio plays eighties hits. *Mama se mama sa ma ma coo sa.* The gentle weave of our small talk is comforting, our collective tasks simple and repetitive. I unpeel the plastic wrap from a multipack of tinned tuna. I squint at the neck of a vegetable oil bottle, where the sell-by date is etched like a secret message. Heavy crates are lifted onto and off scales. We fall into the trance of busywork, paying quiet homage to our dumb and lovely fingers, the efficiency of our joints. I don't have to be brilliant, talented or articulate here, merely useful.

There are, I trust, people feeding those who haven't means, who quietly share what they have not out of charity but the simple fact of familiarity. They give because they, too, have been hungry and cold, mortified at the gnawing, endless needs of their bodies. Charity is different. Charity as a principle and an ethic tends to appeal to those with plenty. This redistributive approach makes sense in a world where the gap between the haves and have-nots is so vast. But it means the act of giving is warped by the biases and preferences of the wealthy. They decide the terms and parameters of their own kindness, to whom and how it is given.

If you are determined to find it, there is always some lack that renders you unable to give to others. There is a magical, unspecified amount of money at which all material need and lack supposedly disappears and frees you to think of others. Wealthy people talk all the time about 'giving back'. The problem with this is it assumes that one must reach a certain point of plenitude to then have something to offer. This one-sided model, where one party gives and the other gratefully and wordlessly accepts, is broken.

It's an impossible goal: complete equality across all lines. But an attempt at reciprocity feels like a good thing to aim for. A mutual giving whose scope goes beyond the material but necessarily understands the urgency of our base needs. How might we cultivate and even enjoy a need for each other, outside the assumed strictures of intimate relationships? Most people like the idea of giving to charity, but it's rare to find the person who doesn't feel at least a flicker of shame at accepting it. We know, instinctually, that there is a hierarchy, one that turns the receiver into a lesser, more abject human. Though they may get the things they need 'for free', they often pay in dignity and privacy, their right to be anything other than obsequiously grateful.

Like many celebrities of his stature, Michael was a huge philanthropist, donating millions to various charities over his lifetime. He was especially generous to charities working with children. During world tours, he would visit children's hospitals and when back home in Neverland, a steady stream of children would visit the grounds. These invitations continued even after the first spate of allegations in 1993 and right up until Martin Bashir's pivotal documentary *Living with Michael Jackson* in 2003.

He seemed to want, more than anything, to be one of these kids. Mutual need, equal risk. But he wasn't. He was a multi-millionaire, an adult man, the biggest pop star in the world. No amount of giving can absorb someone unfathomably rich into the same world as those they help. The way money, having too much or not enough of it, shapes our experience of each other makes harder work of the already daunting task of genuine connection. The loneliness and maladjustment that plagued Michael, and ultimately became his foil for the abuse he committed, is an extreme and specific kind. The twinned isolation and narcissism of the hyper-rich and famous, though hard to sympathise with for most of us, is a powerful allegory for how persistent feelings of distance can warp how we relate to each other. Too many of us, through no fault of our own, know nothing but power exchange, the varying positions of deference and dominance.

Michael declared himself 'the loneliest person in the world' – even in this confession of existential despair, there is megalomania. He believed his loneliness complete and overwhelming, of a magnitude deeper and wider than anyone else could possibly conceive. In his autobiography, he described how he would 'walk through my neighbourhood hoping I'd run into somebody I could talk to and perhaps become friends with. I wanted to meet people who didn't know who I was.'

Loneliness convinces its owner that their pain is unprecedented, specifically ruinous and without end. It is the pitiful and dangerous belief that humans must coerce, manipulate or bully each other to get what they need. Intense self-loathing and narcissism are two sides of the same coin, an excessive and compulsive self-regard that smothers any notion that many of your fellow human beings are just as complex and wanting as you.

I have made a proud ornament of my solitude, pruned and cared for it at the expense of the larger project of togetherness. The truth is that I fear people. The magnitude of their wants and foibles overwhelms me. It is easier to look from a distance, to float in and out of obligation on a fickle tide. Many social arrangements are passed off as community: friendship cliques, niche interest groups, online forums, even brands have co-opted the language of community. But community born of proximity is elusive, receding into the distance after our school days are over and we've left our family homes. People who never leave the town they grew up in are often framed as pitiful, doomed to the shrinking of inexperience. But more and more, I am struck by what we lose as our worlds expand, how the infinite possibility of connections curses us to sow seed after seed of potential but never to tend, to observe, to fix what is present rather than destroy what unnerves us and continually start again.

It is precisely when I have sat too long in the literal echo chamber of my own living room, my self-obsessed thoughts running laps around the room, that I have felt the most fearful and spiteful. I hear the shouts through the wall and imagine a monstrous mother who ought to be dragged out in the street and made to face our judging eyes. Her children, I tell myself, are already lost causes, doomed to be cruel parents and partners, passing trauma down the generations like a rusting baton. This story is neat and rigid, comforting in its firm corners. I do not knock on their door, do not risk knowing their faces or learning their names. I guard my righteousness, my unanchored spite.

Neverland

In the 1987 video for 'Leave Me Alone', Michael sails through a cavernous fairground of delights and horrors. Amongst its population are Labradors in suits, the dancing bones of the Elephant Man, a set of snapping false teeth. There is even a cameo from a wide-eyed Elizabeth Taylor who floats across the screen like a listless Miss Havisham. This video is not as iconic as some of his others, but it's aged remarkably well. On a revisit, it reveals itself as sophisticated and experimental, ripe with symbols that have only grown in potency.

The video is a literal collage, pieced together by director Jim Blashfield over nine months. Its maximalism reminds me of the many times I sat cross-legged on the floor with a glue stick, scissors and a stack of magazines, lost in a composite world of my own making. Collage is an idealistic medium that forces incongruent images into a new context. Charged with their own lateral logic, once unrelated images create their own universe. It feels good to play god, to keep what we like and discard what we don't.

This funfair scene reads like an early blueprint for the behemoth that would become the Neverland Ranch. Michael bought the fully furnished residence and land from real estate developer William Bone in 1988 and named it after the fabled home of Peter Pan.

The novelty of money that can be spent on one's whims rather than spent on the bare bones of survival is dizzying. The itch to indulge the child in us is strong, no matter how advanced in years we may be. I remember, for example, the first time I could spend ten whole pounds on whatever I wanted in the school tuck shop. I walked out with two white paper bags straining from their contents. With the last ten minutes of my break, I folded an endless concertina of fizzy laces into my face until the saliva in my throat thickened to sugar paste. I chased the initial pleasure of the sugar hit even as it receded and the synthetic taste of strawberry turned sickly. The gelatine glued my teeth together and still I couldn't stop. It was not a matter of if I should keep going, but that I could.

These are the regressive choices of the newly endowed and unrestrained. The child inside us still wailing for the things they were denied is hard to ignore. Adulthood is, hopefully, realising that not only can we not have what we want at all times, but that even if we could, that life would be a grotesque distortion, rendering joyful things tedious or even repellent. Neverland has its own nullification baked into the name. It is a childish attempt to have it all, all the time. It would prove to be a Faustian bargain for which Michael and the children he kept in his orbit would pay dearly.

The ranch was a refuge from not only the paparazzi but a balm for the wounds of deferred childhood. But Neverland also operated as a covert PR campaign for Michael as Big Kid. Everything about it was built to appeal to the young children whose company he sought. The gamut of visitors ran from child stars like Macaulay Culkin to unknown kids with a litany of social and medical woes, who, of course, were dazzled by Neverland's splendour. He offered tours of the house for large groups of children, favouring the sick and terminally ill. He paid for hospital bills, gave extravagant gifts of cars and money to starry-eyed carers and parents. It must have felt like a miracle to a parent besieged by worry and debt, the King of Pop opening the gates to a place of impossible dreams. A dream of a sick child healed, poverty deferred, the drudge of normality waved away with the flick of a wand.

Neverland is a great example of what writer Kate Wagner catalogues in her blog McMansion Hell. She describes the architecture of a typical McMansion as 'designed in order to cram the most "features" inside for the lowest costs. These features exist to increase the house's resale value, not to make it a good place to live. No thought is given to the labor needed to clean and maintain these spaces. The master bathroom includes intricate stone surfaces that can only be scrubbed with a toothbrush; the cathedral ceilings in the living room raise the heating and cooling costs to an exorbitant sum; the chandelier in the grand entryway dangles so high that no one can replace the bulbs in it, even with a stepladder.'

In the years leading up to Michael's death in 2009, he was rumoured to be on the brink of bankruptcy. Maintaining Neverland was no doubt an ever-growing burden on his finances. Like many down-at-heel stars before him, the ill-fated This Is It tour read like a cash grab to keep the star and his estate afloat. A house intended to be a magical haven away from the pressures of public opinion and accountability was now a daily reminder of the undeniable waning of his wealth and power. After the FBI raided Neverland for evidence in the wake of the second wave of allegations, Michael left Neverland and never returned again.

Neverland began as unbridled wish fulfilment and collapsed

into a museum of former glory and, finally, a den of hidden horrors. A house built in service to self-mythology is always doomed to crumble. If Michael's childhood home in Gary is the beginning of a fairy tale, then Neverland is its ambivalent conclusion. I suspect I'm not the only person to build my adult notions of a home on what I felt I lacked as a child. Add fame and excessive riches to this, and what became of Michael seems less unfortunate and more inevitable.

I confess I do not believe in time. I like to fold my magic carpet, after use, in such a way as to superimpose one part of the pattern upon another. Let visitors trip.

—Vladimir Nabokov

Home is a place I am always en route to. I scarcely know when I've landed there, don't know if I'd recognise its door or facade. My most vivid memories are being ferried from one place to the next, the relief of suspension. When I was on my way to somewhere, I could live in multiple realities, luxuriate in potential. In the passenger seat of a car, nothing was settled or resolved. In the boot of the car were all the things I needed to get by. Later, I would learn this was the same nomadic itch of the backpacker and commitment-phobe, the culturally and socially exiled. But, as a kid, I just knew that I liked how songs sounded with the motion of wheels under me, that staying in any place was tolerable knowing I was never stuck anywhere for long.

Behind my eyelids, a slideshow plays of everywhere I've ever laid my head: the home of the Gujarati childminder whose floor was a squeaky lino etched with a pattern of intricate squares. The sofa and remote control were wrapped in sticky-back plastic. There was a tiny bubble of air by the mute button that I worried with my finger, a precursor to my later love for picking spots. Clive's home was WWF on loud in the living room, a cracked leather settee pummelled flat by our feet as we flung ourselves to the floor like the wrestlers onscreen. The procession of well-off friends from secondary school, whose homes I spent many days in, had houses made of traditional brick and dark, whorled wood. Any given room smelt of woodsmoke or fresh bread. The kitchens gleamed and the old-fashioned Agas meant the kitchens were always warm. I loved the wooden beams of one particular girl's house the most, marvelling at how they ribbed the ceiling like a pirate vessel.

I felt, naively, we lived incidental to and outside our surroundings. Our bonding as friends was instant and pure despite, or maybe because of, how circumstantial it was. We just wanted to watch DVDs and eat junk food in peace, giggle into our palms and conjecture about our future fantasy lives. This could be done anywhere, in any house with a roof and a sofa, a TV in a convenient place.

Yet: I only had a friend visit my house once. I don't remember the details of it, only that it never happened again. Whether an explicit conversation happened, I can't recall, but it was understood that I was someone who visited people's houses. People did not visit mine. Our homes can feel like secrets we don't even know we're keeping. When certain people cross the threshold, what feels normal, functional and familiar is suddenly shameful and inadequate in the eyes of the visitor in your midst. It did not matter if this was reality or fearful projection. Home was a site of trial, where one's intricate rituals and failures were laid bare for others to assess.

Before I crossed the threshold of other people's homes, the homes of my family were the world. Their ways and norms were all there had been or will ever be. What reason was there to think otherwise? But, as I got older I learnt to adopt an implicit secretiveness. Our parents or caregivers tell us things about themselves and the world that don't add up, or start to rub up against the things we hear out there, in the wider world. We are not told explicitly to be ashamed or furtive, but we see it in the shifts. Different foods are cooked for guests, a mother's voice goes up two octaves as she talks to other parents.

The accumulative ways that the world outside and the one inside don't add up lead to this first, formative sense of dissonance. The first time I visited a friend's house, I felt it. The unnerving reality of other people's divergent lives, happening right alongside yours. People put their furniture in different places. Their rooms are different sizes, their walls painted in jarring colours. They might call their dinner tea or supper, eat it much later or earlier than you do. Dinner at a table, not perched laps on a sunken sofa. Some families exchange anecdotes about their day, others fling insults and crockery at each other. It's an uncomfortable dawning that your home may not fit other people's definition, that if someone else's family is the supposed standard, then yours is, by default, defective.

So even as the horrors of some living situations become apparent, there is a need to defend one's turf. Though none of us choose where and to whom we're born, to be criticised for our home life can feel like we are being condemned. That's why so many of us find ourselves defending the indefensible, shielding our families from the scrutiny of outsiders. It is too painful to be judged by others who observe from a safe distance, who don't live as we do and inevitably measure our situation from the eyes of the distant voyeur. Statistics show that most abuse happens in the home, in familiar surroundings and amongst family members who know and claim to care for each other. Home becomes a site of many nevers, the place hardest to betray to the scrutiny and condemnation of others.

Home Is Where the Heart Is, Home Is Where the Hurt Is

Of all the places I called home, I revisit Auntie and Uncle E's the most. The soft, frosted green carpet, the crater left by Uncle's weight in the sofa where he sat to watch the boxing, how I tracked where Auntie was in the house by the sound of the slap-slap-slap of her slippers against her heels echoing from one room to the next.

Uncle was always asking provocative questions, quick with an opinion and keen for a debate. Leaning in close, he taps his head with the barrel of two fingers. *Let me tell you something about this life, okay*. His advice was always something about winners never quitting, triumph over your enemies, boilerplate phrases from the sweaty Pentecostal TV preachers he watched on Sundays. Auntie rolled her eyes and told me to ignore him. But, always, a smile twitched at her lips. She found him charming despite herself. I did, too.

Uncle was fun and he was funny. I loved his tall tales, the hyena-like hiss of his laugh. Sometimes, he'd drive me to the bookshop, fold a twenty-pound note in my hand and tell me to pick whatever I wanted. On a shelf full of books in their house, he owned just two. A black leather King James Bible and a biography of Frank Bruno. Still, he insisted that the key to a sharp brain and a good life was to read.

When Auntie was in one of what Uncle called her 'storm clouds', we would leave her at home and take long drives down the local high street, passing a string of chicken shops, betting dens and newsagents and on to a retail park. Oh, how I loved the retail park, its brash colours and the long, yawning aisles inside the bargain shops. All those cars dutifully moving through the clogged arteries of roundabouts, the satisfying grid of parking spaces painted on the asphalt. We'd go to the cash and carry, where Uncle would buy fat bags of rice and massive bottles of vegetable oil. I insisted on helping, though I would need to drop what I was carrying and stop every few steps. He would tease me that I wouldn't last long back in Kampala, where kids half my age easily lift bottles twice the size across great distances.

All his siblings had to work the land, but as the eldest, Uncle had to work the hardest. Every day, he said, he got up before the sun to water crops and gather maize, perfecting the right angle to hit the stalk with his machete so the maize fell on the first strike. He would then go to school with his younger brother. His parents took great pride in having money to pay for them both to go. He liked maths, but nothing else interested him. At least when he was on his father's land, the results of hard work were visible and immediate. Food, his father's respect, a satisfying ache in the muscles. His sisters would help with feeding the younger siblings, cleaning the house, preparing food for the evening meal.

The life he described was hard for me to imagine. I'd never

sown a seed or swung a hoe into soil. The thought of such an existence, how it rubbed against what I'd been told made life valuable, frightened and embarrassed me. How soft and indulged his stories made me feel, how utterly divorced from the earth and its mechanics.

Uncle didn't talk about his mother much, especially after she died. It was his father who came up repeatedly, a man I'd seen in one or two sepia-toned photos. He had eyes drooped at the corners, a stern mouth that looked like it smiled rarely. He looked regal and weary in the photo, hands clasped tight in his lap. His wife, my jjajja, is stood behind him with her hands resting on the back of his chair, the starched sleeves of her gomesi dress pointing proud as arrows.

'Did your father beat you?' I asked, though I already suspected the answer. I imagined Uncle as a smiley, smooth-skinned boy, hair shaved close to his protruding skull. In his hand a football dyed by the red earth, once-white hexagons the colour of parchment. Skinny, vital, eyes alive to the street in front of him. Maybe the constant scanning of his environment is the search for his father, the ever-present tension of possible punishment.

The scene fades before I can find any of this evidence. Now, in the car, Uncle's large hands confidently manoeuvre the wheel and the gear stick. I cannot imagine him cowering or fearful, at the mercy of some force larger than himself. I would come to know that Uncle, and so many Uncles like him, lived lives of muted terror, first from their fathers, then the indifferent island forever poised to spit them out. Rare was the man I met of their generation who did not continue this legacy, who knew no other way but to cut through the stalks of life with the crass slice of a machete.

When I'm old I'll go back, he told me. He meant to Kampala, but he seemed to want to go back to a life where the line between cause and consequence was simpler. That I couldn't understand, feeling saddled as I did by the adults around me who got to choose where I went, who I saw and what I ate. But here was Uncle, driving his own car in the promised land, wanting to go back to collecting empty bottles and cutting maize with his father behind him.

I had dominion over the car stereo, could pick the soundtrack of our journey. Uncle's favourite MJ album was *Dangerous*, and so we'd play that on repeat. I liked the insistent New Jack Swing of 'Jam'. Uncle liked the moody rock of 'Give In To Me', which featured Slash on guitar. That difference in our favourite tracks gave us licence to pay more attention to each other's tastes. Soon, I loved 'Give In To Me'. I had listened to it with especial care, listening for what Uncle might love about it. Letting the music fill the car was a relief from wondering what to say on these journeys. I had some mythical vision of how family ought to talk to each other, the conversation I assumed flowed without pause in every other car that passed us. Thank god for music, how reliable and mutual it was. Where words failed, bopping our heads to a song we both loved sufficed.

There was not a lot my family seemed to be bonded by or agreed on. We were each, in subtle, unforgivable ways, illegible to each other. There were silences, huge gaps in the story of how and why we were that were never revealed to me. This seemed, at the time, a chosen cruelty on their part. Now, I see a cluster of migrants mired in their own aftershocks, forced to build community in a country that barely tolerated their presence, wanted them quiet, compliant, backs bent in deathly gratitude.

The nuclear family, in its two-up two-down cocoon, was the fixed and rightful definition of home. The rest of us, who didn't want or couldn't have this, were deviants by default. I spent years feeling condemned by my family's inability to love and live how I thought they should. Now I question the norms by which we were always doomed to fail. When I try to decipher a unifying principle between us, marooned in all of our separate dreams and disappointments, it's clear we were all linked by one thing. Like kids believe in the Tooth Fairy and Father Christmas, we loved and believed in Michael. Everything else aside, for that I am grateful. To that, I choose to hold on.

For the first time in over five years, I am at Auntie E's house. The carpet is the same colour, the CDs and vinyl still stacked where I remember them. Auntie has shrunk, though. Or maybe I have grown taller. These places that once felt vast, full of things yet to traverse, feel small and provincial when we return. All the music in this room, and more, is easily accessible now, contained in the smartphones we carry like stubborn tics. I do not wake up every day in giddy awe at this technological wonder, the impossible joy of having the Alexandria Library in my back pocket. The kid who stared at the vastness of all there was to hear and marvelled is gone.

The flat is silent as I walk in. It was never like this before. Music would be heard as soon as the front door opened, all down the short hallway into the living room. In the kitchen, Radio 4 presenters delivered the shipping forecast in their gentle RP undulations. Feel free to play something, if you want, she offers. But it doesn't feel right. I turn the kettle on and make us both a cup of tea. Her slow, considered steps worry me. She has long stopped doing anything elaborate to her hair. Under a yellow scarf poke the ends of two fuzzy plaits. Her baby hairs are sparse, dusted with grey. I feel like Alice, one moment too large, the next too small.

The boxes propped against the wall are all different sizes, already scrawled with words crossed out but still legible. *Fragile: Plates and Bowls*, one says. *Books. Music. Photos.* When you buy a lamp, a book or a record with a shared life in mind, there is such hope, the brave assumption of love's exponential growth. You don't dare think of how the end might arrive, suddenly or in subtle, seamless increments, until there is a stack of flattened boxes propped against a wall, a division of assets made in silence.

Auntie is moving to another, smaller flat. She has shown me pictures. It is sleek and modern, with a grey floor made to look like wood. It's the soulless interior of a budget hotel, but I tell her it looks great. I can't imagine her walking around that sterile space, her toes no longer bristled by this hideous, homely green carpet. She is set on only keeping enough CDs and vinyl to fit in one box. The rest will be donated to the local charity shop. We sort them together, me sat on the floor and Auntie on a stiff-backed chair to support her achy back. We are accompanied by the shuffles and clicks of CD cases and vinyl sleeves, the screech of parcel tape.

Auntie holds a record for a minute, exhales a soft, sad laugh. She shows me the cover: Michael in a sherbet-yellow shirt, the lens frosted in that quintessentially eighties sheen. It was as if everything that happened in that decade was wreathed in an aerosol haze. 'Rock With You', the song her and Uncle would two-step to when Auntie was in a good mood. I smile at the memory, silently nurse the quick stab of sadness that follows. The album was a gift from Uncle, the first thing he bought her when they arrived in England. A quick flash of his face visits me, vivid and welcome. We swap memories of him, as if we are at his wake.

Later, she takes off her headscarf and undoes one of her plaits, parts the hair to show me a bald patch on her head the size of a golf ball. I knew it was there. I'd spotted it once as I'd watched her combing and greasing her hair. For the most part she hid it well, arranging her braids to one side or wrapping her head in one of her pretty silk scarves. I'd never thought to ask about it, assuming it was some genetic quirk, an experiment with relaxer gone wrong. She breathes out, like she's been holding the breath in for years.

Uncle was driving fast one night, she said. *He often drove when he was tipsy, but this time he was slurring words, driving through red lights.* Her finger patiently felt for the edge of the tape, put another box together. *I had on this beautiful dress*, she says. *I'd taken my shoes off, they were pinching me. The ground was freezing. It had been snowing, I think. He was shouting and shouting, stupid man. I told him to shut up and wait until we got home. All those people in their fancy houses could hear us.* She rips the next piece of tape with her teeth, laughs her own private laugh. *Oh, it was a nice dress, Vanessa. Purple. Real silk. Back when you could get good-quality things from the market, not like now. And he was dragging me down the street in it.*

Turns out someone did hear and called the police. She did the talking while Uncle sat quietly in the car, the tuft of hair he pulled from her head in her balled fist. They got away with a caution. I had had no idea, not even the ghost of an inkling that Uncle had done this. I knew they'd had their issues, grown-up dynamics that I chose not to pry into. But nothing like this. Dear god, I never thought it was as bad as this. I feel awful for all the times I resented her moods, the moments I preferred Uncle for being fun, berated her for being sensible. I put my arms around her, and she lets me. We sit for a while, Auntie looking out at the small pile of taped boxes, years of her life shut away, labelled. We sit quietly in the room that grew me, the room where Uncle held me and Auntie fed me and Uncle hit her and we all broke ourselves with happiness listening to Michael Jackson.

I have that dress somewhere, still. You should have it. You'd look good in it.

Auntie is busy in the kitchen, deep cleaning. My mind is slow and stupid, her story not slotting into place. Uncle, fun uncle, Uncle with the magic wallet and the silly jokes and the handles that plucked the dead leaves so gently from the bushes. My favourite uncle, who bought me and my cousins the best Christmas gifts, whose thumbs had so gently wiped at my cheeks when I cried my childish tears. This same uncle had dragged Auntie through the street like a sacrificial goat. My rage is too late, too impotent. It is done. All of this has already been lived, survived, accepted. He had been all these things simultaneously, each version existing in its own layer. And now she is leaving him, not because of violence or hurt or righteous indignation, but a quiet exhaustion.

She passes me a Millie Jackson record for the donation box. I sense that if I press for more, she won't continue. Part of me is glad she isn't. What use does she have for my retrospective anger, my naive appeals to a past that can't be changed? I don't get to tell her what to do with her pain. But we are here now, several steps into the truth's tide. There is nowhere left to go but further in.

Do you hate him? I ask.

Auntie shakes her head, waves her hand as if batting away a fly.

Finally, she said: *How can I hate him? He took care of me.*

And instead of saying the truth, that I couldn't bring myself to hate him either, I become angry with her. She was not presenting the clear, bracing victimhood that I need, the anger that would give me the bravery to renounce my Uncle. If she asked me, I would have done it. But she does not want that. She wants to move on with her life, change the record and start again.

We finish packing the music, dismantle the CD racks and move the cabinets. On the wall, pale squares mark their absence, shocks of almost white against magnolia. They look like phantom doorways I might wander through and return to my six-year-old self, Auntie and Uncle together. At some point I can't pinpoint, nostalgia stopped feeling like a warm, softened glow on fond memories and more like the slow creep of dread. I heard that nostalgia used to be considered an illness that could kill, back when it was defined as a pining for home rather than a bygone moment. It would be listed on the death certificates of soldiers: *homesickness*. As I watched Auntie's face wince at the memory each album cover unleashed, it made sense to me that people returned alive from the unnameable horrors of physical combat, only for the hauntings of a fabled home to kill them.

As I leave, Auntie gives me a big hug. Her body feels pleasantly soft and full in my arms. She presses my face between her hands like she used to when I was little. *Call him* she says. *I bet he misses you.*

A year after Auntie and Uncle split, he calls and insists on taking me for a birthday dinner.

We go to Wagamama, where Uncle stabs at his chicken gyoza with one chopstick, table manners as graceless as they ever were. He repeats jokes that he's been telling for years, viscerally slurps his food, tells me that he's taking up kickboxing at the gym to get fit. Many minutes hang together, where I do not think of It.

Then it happens, often in the brief moments where he seems the most unguarded and vulnerable. As he polishes his glasses on his fleece, it will flash hot and quick through my head. Hands wrapped round hair, the blue lights of a police car. The hem of Auntie's dress, dark, wet. Bloodied scalp, silent drive. In the time it takes for him to put his glasses back on, it's gone.

I know I will never ask him about it. I'm convinced he does not know what he did. He would deny it if I confronted him because his brain will do what brains do. It will rewrite, reframe or completely shut out the truth of what he did. And even if he acknowledged it, what then? I chew my noodles, burn my tongue on the broth. I drink my gin and tonic. I seethe. As the waiter puts the bill on the table, Uncle claps a hand on my shoulder and squeezes, asks me what I'm writing. A book about Michael Jackson, I say. The one and only King of Pop! he says, smiling. Can you still moonwalk? I shake my head, laugh. Odd. I can't remember the last time I attempted it. He tells me he is proud of me. As always, he pays.

He offers me a lift to the train station, where I will take the hour-and-fifteen-minute journey back to my empty flat, think my irresolvable thoughts alone. It strikes me that I want to walk into a physical place of other grief-ravaged people and burrow my way into some kind of work, an audacious grasp at something more interesting, more thorough, more humane than condemnation or coddling.

I may have to leave language here, at this impasse where it cannot take me further. The indicator in Uncle's new company car ticks like a metronome. He does not remind me to put on my seatbelt like he always used to; his new car does it for him with an ellipsis of bleeps. Even as he's sat beside me, I miss him. I will never again sit across from him in the passenger seat innocent of what he did – and, for all I know, still does.

Growing older is not the blooming of wisdom everybody promised. What I feel instead is a waning, the growing inability to trust my ears, my eyes, my fickle instincts. On the phone nudging my pocket, a never-ending menu of conspiracy theories and alternative realities and reactions to reactions to the news cycle of climate crisis and economic freefall and chronic isolation.

A now free Britney posts videos of herself spinning manically in tiny bikini bottoms, alone in her cavernous kitchen, repeating dance routines she perfected while still too young to drink. Clive comes home every year, an inch broader in the shoulders, quieter and quieter. Eyes like trapdoors. My godson's teeth push through his gums, and we tell him, again and again, not to pull or grab or push, though he's still too young to grasp the impact of his hands. After a long time of not being able to, I listen to Michael's music again. It still sets my synapses alight.

Yes, I dance under a faint shadow of sadness, but I have banished guilt. I have no use for the false propeller of that feeling. I am tired of its self-obsessed, circular dance. But I don't want to live in the colourless world where Michael and his music don't exist. I believe, greedily, that I can have this and a world where less of us are subject to unnecessary pain and humiliation. I have made my peace that others will disagree, and hope their choices serve them as mine do me. I don't know if these principles can sit side by side, which is why I am trying it. I cannot report on feasibility just yet. Come back to me on my deathbed for my verdict. All I can say for sure is I am not afraid of being wrong. I am not afraid of being human.

In the car I notice Uncle has shrunk since I last saw him. He smacks his middle proudly, makes a joke about Auntie's weight, the growing apron of her stomach over her jeans. The two of them still talk, seem to get on much better than they did for years before they ended things. As he continues talking about Auntie's body, I wait for the engine of rage to rev up, the numbing bliss of denial. Neither shows up.

He is my favourite Uncle. He will die someday, and I know I will mourn him. Will that sadness overshadow my need for his punishment, his reckoning? I suspect this is the fortress that all violence rests on. It's this collective paralysis that keeps me in mute deflection and denial. I choose to look determinedly ahead at the road in front of me, in the fear that if I stopped, if I spoke out loud what I see and feel, everything would unravel. I would not survive all the tiny and fatal ways I've betrayed the people I love and betrayed myself.

Uncle starts the engine. We share a silence for several minutes until I can't bear the thud of my thoughts. I reach for the radio dial and the brief reprieve of the music. I am safe here for the time being, in a car, on my way, sitting with what I've left behind and the hopeful mirage of what's ahead. Not happy and not sad, not minor or major. A suspended chord between two lands of certainty. I live there, in a land I've never dared to explore until now.

Come find me there, if you like.

Dear Michael

Here's what might have happened –
you, five years old, open your mouth and a sound falls out,
to no applause, no cheers,
it hovers, no more or less celebrated
than a passing bird's,
your father rests in the next room,
the frowning face of his father
at the edge of all his dreams,
fearsome, fleeting, then forgiven

you trace the grooves of the windowsill,
send a sigh up to the ceiling
(i wish you the gift of boredom)
perhaps you tap a rhythm out, jig your shoulders,
you move as it pleases you,
no mirrors to chide you,
no false idols to mimic from the wings,
and if someone were to see, they might say,
you were pretty good, but not great,
nothing special
(i wish you the gift of averageness)
I imagine you remarkably unremarkable,
faintly wistful for fame and fortune

I tell myself this would have made the difference

What is the alternative?
the flat horror of cruelty
we can never escape
common and fickle as wind

What is the alternative?

I would have to rescind my love
and own my cowardice

sometimes and suddenly
i am so murderous with anger
my throat eats itself and
my nails choke on dirt

how could you how could you how could you
short of wrenching your body out of that
villainous ingot of a coffin they buried you in
shaking a confession from your corpse

i don't know what else to do
but imagine:

a young black boy at the beginning of himself
nose and eyes and smile like
a brother i might have had in some other life
unfurling beneath this one
a brother who might sing for the simple
pleasure of his own voice
fizzing inside his mouth

who might hear the sound of his name
(my-call, my-call)
from the next room and
wonder where that sound
comes from, so gentle
and loving and so very
faint, like a song half remembered
a melody that belongs to nothing
but itself and the gentle boy who
hums it

ACKNOWLEDGEMENTS

Shan't lie, folks: writing this book broke my brain a bit. It might be a while until I fully recover. Many times, I didn't think I'd finish, but finish I did! I've long known that having one name on the front of a book belies the collaborative effort of any published work, but now I know it in my bones.

There's no way this book would exist without the people I'm about to shout out. To any aspiring writers reading this, please know it's no weakness to lean on others in your process. With every day that goes by, I am learning that we really do *need* each other in all that we do, and writing is no exception. The figure of the solitary genius is a lie, no more than a marketing gimmick. Books are made by many hands and many minds, and the ones that brought mine into being are pretty special. *★insert airhorns★* Here they are, in all their glory.

To my agent and fellow MJ fan Becky Thomas, thank you for championing this book and for representing me, and all us weirdo poets, all these years. I am very proud to be presented by you, a working-class woman with her own independent agency. Thank you for holding all the hats I wear as an artist and finding the spaces for me to thrive.

Thank you to the whole team at Canongate for your

immediate enthusiasm about this book, to Hannah Knowles for your belief and Helena Gonda for swiftly and brilliantly taking up the helm halfway through. You are a kind, meticulous and infinitely patient editor. Thank you for weathering my many storms of self-doubt and missed deadlines (!) and asking me the right questions at the right times. Thank you to Alison Rae, whose eagle-eyed copy-edit and warm, open-minded and intelligent manner over the phone helped push me over the finish line. I hope we get to work together again soon. Here's to the long walk towards wisdom.

Max motherfucking Porter. For some reason, off a Twitter DM, you agreed to read the earliest scraps of this book, and your faith in me and this book often kept me going when little else did. Thank you for your insight, your bracing honesty, your humour, your humility, that remarkably open, uncynical heart of yours. I aspire just as much to your caring and principled nature as I do your obscene brilliance as a writer.

To Tash, my dear friend, confidante and mother to my beloved godson: thank you for leaving me bagels at the bottom of my stairs when I couldn't bear to leave the house and lending me your laptop when I accidentally baptised mine, scream. Thank you for your support, your calm, your insistence on the restorative properties of *Married at First Sight*. What you and Tommy have built together remains the best example I know of love in its purest form. Thank you for letting me be a part of your wonderful family.

To Mim, thank you for your fierce, beautiful brain, your faith in the floundering first draft I sent you, the impromptu flowers, the years we spent in blind faith we'd one day make a career from this writing malarkey. Look at us now! Thank you for being the whetstone on which I sharpen my thoughts, the person I can always rely on to dig under all the pleasantries and platitudes to the dark, grisly heart of the matter. You are CANON and I am very proud to know and love you.

To Torres, the smartest, kindest, most principled and precious person I know. You are too good for this world, so we must make the world better for you. MWIML.

To Rebecca Tantony, to Kavina Minhas, to Francie Clark, to Bridget Minamore, to Toby Campion, to Temi Wilkey, to Ngaio Aniya and Sarah Bickerton – thank you for your friendship. I adore and admire you all immensely.

Thank you to my writer friends who read early proofs and/or offered much-needed advice, encouragement and laughter now and in the past: Nikesh Shukla, Travis Alabanza, Candice Carty Williams, Caleb Femi, Nathan Filer, Will Harris, Amy Key, Salena Godden, Hollie McNish, Deanna Rodger, Otegha Uwaba, Shon Faye, Inua Ellams, George Kelly and Matt Rowland Hill. Gassed and honoured to have you all as peers and pals.

Thank you to the poetry community that built me and all the amazing friends I've made there. Thank you to Burning Eye for being the first press to publish me and all the people who've booked me to yell poems from a stage. Thanks for feeding my confidence and also my latent narcissist streak. Whoops.

Thank you to Hawkwood for giving me a place to focus on the book for a week and every person and place that's paid me to write, think, speak or perform over the past fourteen years. Each of those opportunities brought me to this point and I take none of it for granted.

Thank you to the many writers who have shown me that the task of writing is both an aesthetic and moral endeavour: Toni Morrison, James Baldwin, Susan Sontag, Ben Lerner, Hanif Abdurraqib, Saidiya Hartman and Dionne Brand to name but a few. I am a writer because I am a reader, and in my many moments of sadness, confusion, loneliness and despair, the rigorous words of brilliant minds have kept me company, offered me solace and filled me with courage.

Big up, Grace! Big up, Nina! Big up, Janelle!

Thank you, Mum, thank you, Dad. My awe and respect for you only grows as the years go by.

Thank you to my Bristol Ballroom fam for your defiant, queer joy and how much it has fed, affirmed and educated me. You are the future.

And, finally, to Michael. Your music is one of my favourite things about being alive. I am trying my best to contribute to a world where talent and influence like yours doesn't have to lead to exploitation and abuse. You were failed by those you trusted, and you failed those who trusted you. Regardless: thank you for the music and thank you for the memories.